READ THIS BOOK BEFORE
YOU GO TO PRESS

"Self Publishing is not for the faint of heart. I strongly urge you to **read this book before you go to press.**"
—Earl Cox, Publisher—*Writersandpoets.com, LLC*

The African American's Guide to Successful Self Publishing is a refreshing read on self publishing one's book that invokes high interest, and challenges the author-to-be to gain professional composure before writing The Book. Shocking truths of **what it takes to succeed in the highly competitive world of publishing** are told from a fresh new voice on the topic, but who has many years of professional experience as an editor for major magazines. Read it to avoid rejection of your manuscript and be on your way to honing and fine-tuning a quality book that you'll be proud of.
—Heather Covington, Publisher, *Disilgold, Inc.*

African American Writers Guide to Successful Self Publishing is a pragmatic primer to prepare you for the world of publishing—especially self-publishers. This practical guide provides step-by-step information to help you run a successful business. This is **a must-read for those who want to take the self-publishing plunge**
—Pat Byrdsong, Former Vice President, Black Women In Publishing and Editor, *True Confessions* magazine

Writing is a difficult and arduous process. It takes the discipline and patience that many people don't have. In this book, **Ms. Powell** takes you through the process step-by-step which **eases the anxiety writing creates.**
—Marcia Y. Mahan—Editor, *JIVE* magazine

FINALLY! A BOOK FOR ASPIRING AUTHORS!...with all the information to guide new authors through the process...from the beginning to the end. Now, they can self-publish their own books and get them on the market without any restrictions.

— **Pat Stevenson, Publisher,** *Harlem News Group, Inc.*

As a former editor at *Jive/Intimacy* black romance novels, Powell is well placed to advise new black writers, here **outlining the steps necessary** to get short stories, novels and other works published.

— **Ann Burns, Editor,** *Library Journal*

The African-American Writer's Guide to Successful Self-Publishing:

Marketing, Distribution, Publicity, The Internet... Crafting and Selling Your Book

Takesha D. Powell

Amber Books

Phoenix
New York   Los Angeles

The African-American Writers's Guide to Successful Self-Publishing: Marketing, Distribution, Publicity, The Internet...Crafting and Selling Your Book

Takesha D. Powell

Published by:
Amber Books
A Division of Amber Communications Group, Inc.
1334 East Chandler Boulevard, Suite 5-D67
Phoenix, AZ 85048

Tony Rose, Publisher/Editorial Director   Samuel P. Peabody, Associate Publisher
Yvonne Rose, Senior Editor   The Printed Page, Interior & Cover Design

ALL RIGHTS RESERVED

ISBN#: 0-7394-4887-0

Printed in the U.S.A.

Dedication

For my Mom & Dad,
who've always kept me inspired.

Acknowledgments

First, thanks to Tony Rose and Yvonne Rose who helped me and believed enough in my work to grant me this opportunity. To my parents, my brothers, David and Derrick, all my sisterfriends, Denise, Keisha, Regine, Tonya, Joann, Teresa, Gina, Edna, Adrienne, Hope, to Calvin and my daughter, Dejá who taught me about love and patience.

To Sonia Alleyne, for giving me my first shot at working at a real magazine and getting the experience I needed, the entire staff of Jive/Intimacy magazines. Bloomfield College for the humble beginnings, The Collective Voice, The Aquarian Weekly, Urban Soul Magazine, and City & Suburban Styles magazine.

To Dr. Grace Cornish, you truly inspire me with your strength. And all the magazines that rejected my work at the beginning of my career, it got me here.

About the Author

Takesha Powell, a New York City native is the former Managing Editor of *Black Elegance* and *Belle* magazines as well as former Editor-in-Chief of *Jive/Intimacy* magazines. Ms Powell has two self-published books: an anthology of poetry entitled *Tender Headed: Poems For Nappy Thoughts I Left Uncombed*, and a novel, *The Goode Sisters*. Her next work, *The Sisterhood Commandments: A Novella* is due for release August 2005. She resides both in New York and New Jersey with her daughter.

Introduction

Writing is a process that you've undoubtedly found to be enlightening and rewarding. After having written a number of pages of a manuscript, poem, or short story, you've recently discovered your passion and strength. You've gotten the approval from family and friends who have read your work; and after going to your local poetry club or book reading, you have gained the confidence to take your writing to the next level.

Now you'd like to publicly share your talent with the world and you have spotted a publication that you want to see your work in. If you've purchased this book, you are at the point of finding out how to go about it.

This is a guide for the African-American writer, like you, striving to get short stories, fiction, articles, novels and poetry published or self-published.

When I first began writing, I felt as if it were a secret society that was closed to me. I had submitted to many large, black magazines and book publishers, and was rejected many times, not because my work was bad, but because I didn't have a name in the industry.

As former Managing Editor of *Black Elegance* and *Belle* magazines, I realized how straightforward the publishing industry really is. There were many times when we were looking and anxiously awaiting new writers, often, a seemingly impossible task.

Many of the new writers we hired turned out to be typically unprofessional, unbelievably sloppy and highly unorganized. It was then that it occurred to me that there were many books, manuals and writer's magazines that instructed writers on how to write and how to perfect their craft, but there are not many guides, and certainly no tmany African-American ones, to tell the beginning writer exactly how the publishing process works.

I have provided you with basic information on different marketing avenues for your work, how to write effective query letters and proposals, the art and cost of self-publishing, working with a literary agent and understanding the business of writing, among other highly valuable tips.

This book is for the beginning writer who wishes to begin a new career in the book publishing industry as a published or self-published author.

It was a wise man who said, "Begin at the beginning". And that is what this guide is going to teach you. It is my wish that this book serves to give you confidence to realize that putting your thoughts and ideas down on paper is a true art.

Great things are not promised. They are worked for. I've known many African-American writers who have managed to gain entry to some of the nation's top publishing houses, merely because they believed in themselves and would not give up.

Stay true to your craft and success will follow. The greatest writers have been where you are today. Happy writing!

—Takesha Powell

Contents

To believe in something not yet proved and to underwrite it
with our lives: it is the only way we can leave the future open.
—Lillian Smith

Chapter 1
Why Self-Publish?

Self-publishing can be simplified and put into one word…Freedom. Realistically, though, you may want to publish your own book, novel or poetry collection for any number of reasons.

Reason Number One

You want to have creative freedom to publish ideas that you believe in…whatever is important to you in your life.

Quite often, if you look at books in stores, many of them may sound the same, although you may have submitted similar work to many of those same publishers, only to be repeatedly rejected.

Reason Number Two

You could be self-publishing to have control over your money and to make sure your money isn't being spent towards paying agents and phenomenal publishing costs.

When you know how, where, and what your cash is being spent on, it has a tendency to make you feel more secure and in control of your financial future.

Reason Number Three

You may just wish to publish your work on your own because of the sense of accomplishment it gives you.

To know that you completed a project from beginning to end is an extreme boost for your ego, as well as for your self-esteem. If you're willing to put in the time and dedication towards your project, seeing your work on the bookshelves, in stores, and in libraries will be just that much more liberating.

Hopefully, and more than likely, you'll fall into one or more of these three reasons.

Once you've pinpointed why you choose to go into this process, it will be helpful to use this knowledge throughout your work. In times when you may get discouraged, keeping your reasons in the back of your head will help remind you of why you should keep going.

Stay The Course

It is best to remember that many aspiring writers are dreaming of being published and not everyone will succeed. It is best to keep that in mind always.

The Harsh Reality

Many self-published authors have first tried to get their books published in the mainstream, large publishing houses such as 'Random House' and 'Doubleday'. But, unfortunately, there are far too many novices and poorly skilled writers who are not good at sentence structure or putting together sequences and ideas adequately; and many of those writers will write about something that they have little or no real knowledge about.

Therefore, due to the large volumes of manuscripts they receive—many poorly constructed—it is next to impossible for the editors at major publishing houses to weed through the tons of good work, as well as sorting through the horribly bad work. Thus, with the vast amount of novice writers, large publishers—the publishers that many writers dream of signing with—don't accept unsolicited manuscripts.

2

An unsolicited manuscript is one that has not come through an agent. The normal process requires writers to have an agents to represent them. Your agent is then responsible for pitching your idea to publishers as well as handling financial deals and negotiations.

So, if you don't have an agent when approaching the major publishing houses, you're pretty much left out in the cold because, typically, they will not look at your work.

But, it isn't just as simple as getting an agent and everything is going to be fine. Even if you get one, there are many additional factors to consider, which we will discuss later.

Industry Standards

Besides being overloaded with unsolicited manuscripts and unreputable agents, there is something else that dictates the climate of the publishing industry. And this part is not very attractive.

Something to Think About

Much, not all, but plenty of the industry, is built on copying, to put it bluntly. If your work doesn't have a similar voice to another writer's, then your work is almost guaranteed to get rejected. And this is a big problem in publishing.

You could have a really good manuscript, but the fact of the matter is, major publishers are concerned with what is going to sell and **only** that. I find that many African-American writers use cliché's in their books and even though most African-American imprint books have African-American editors heading them, the books are not representative of us.

In fact, beyond the works that have been centered around up-and-coming, upwardly mobile African-Americans, most of it centers around stereotypical ghetto images. Now there are great African-American writers out here, but there are so many more great stories to tell that are not being heard simply because they don't sound like the current influx of work already in publication.

And that's how it is quite often. When there are shifts in the industry, the books being published change. For a while many novels were humorous, sometimes troubling tales of black women struggling to get a man. Then, a new type of novel showed up on the scene, which explored homosexuality in the black community. These authors were very popular and still are.

The extreme success of Oprah Winfrey's book club pushed more writers to strive for more serious subject matter and many such books gained critical acclaim and instant success.

These are just some of the shifts. Another popular trend, after Terry McMillan's success with *Waiting To Exhale*, was an influx of writers trying to duplicate her work by writing novels about four African-American women and their friendships. Many black men accused these novels of male bashing and emasculating the black male image. Needless to say these were strong trends in the industry. At one time, you could find at least five or six books on the shelves with the same theme, none of them trying to sound drastically different.

And this is not the fault of the writer. There are going to be manuscripts that sound the same, and it is the publishing houses that release books based on current market trends. So it is then, in reality, a marketing ploy, which works, because black books yield generous profits and have loyal followings. So, if the tone and language of your work does not fit what is selling at the time, it's easy to get discouraged.

This may be more than enough encouragement for you to do the "thang" yourself. It is definitely something for you to consider.

Concern For Royalties

This is on the minds of almost every writer. You want to make sure, when your book hits the stands, that you're banking off the amount of money you're due. So in order to make sure you get all the royalties and not some publishing company or your agent, it's best to self-publish.

As with the record industry, there are so many people in a company that stand to profit from you. Therefore, if you don't take the reigns in your own hand, things can get pretty ugly when it comes time for you to collect your money. And that is the reason why self-publishing is quickly becoming the option most new writers seek. Besides the factor discussed previously whereas creativity is a main interest, the money is what's going to pay your bills and allow you to take care of your family when it's all said and done.

After weighing out the pros and cons, it's no wonder so many writers want this control in their lives.

Deadline Concerns

Another reason why a writer may want to self-publish is so that they can have the time they need to get their work out when it suits them. Don't forget that when you work with a publisher, you have a certain amount of time to deliver your manuscript. And once that is delivered to them, it's your editor's job to review what you've submitted to judge whether or not it requires more work or of course, more editing. There may need to be some clarity on your spelling or any slang that you've included.

And, meeting deadlines imposed by someone else can be truly hectic and nerve racking, so it's up to you whether or not you don't mind meeting another person's requirements.

For Example:

Let's say that you lead a pretty fast-paced lifestyle; taking care of kids, a home, your marriage and the barrage of bills that you have to pay; and you can only write a bit here and there everyday. Well, you may be able to get some leniency from your publisher; and then you may not.

Remember that writing is not all about expressing your art, creatively. There are other factors there. The business of writing is a business and time is money to most of us who have to do this day in and day out. So therefore, you are required to be conscious of your deadlines.

I, myself, am no saint and even though I've had plenty of time with deadlines in the past, sometimes I've still failed to deliver on the time I promised. And there was even a delay with me delivering this work on time. Besides my lifestyle being incredibly hectic, I was also incredibly over-worked at my day job, and always at the last minute, I'd find something else I thought I wanted to add to my work. The perfectionist in me also managed to hold things up.

So, if you feel you're unable to meet deadlines and get things done, then it's best that you self-publish and take two to three years, if that's what it takes. But if you do decide to get published by someone else, realize that you should be considerate of his or her time as well. If all else fails and you find yourself being swamped under the various duties of your life, let the publisher know. They may be able to use patience and push the release date of your book back. Sometimes that delay may work out in the end.

However, the schedule is good to be aware of at all times because there are always a series of new writers—with agents—who are waiting to get their book published as well. And, like the seasons that pass with the years, everything has its time and place. When you work with other people, you must fit into their scheme of things.

Industry Changes

As noted previously, there are certain industry standards that dictate whether or not your book gets published. Not only is it frustrating, but it can also defeat your purpose…to get your work out there. But besides this fact, it's hard to keep up with the industry changes.

With the World Trade Center and Pentagon disasters, there has been another shift in the market. No one really knows how long it will last.

But, so far, people are looking for things to make them feel good in this time of uncertainty. People want to get more out of books that are self-help oriented. Books that are going to uplift their spirits and make them relax are the types of things people are looking for.

And people are also looking for ways to change careers, at this point in time. Many of those who were used to having high paid jobs are now at a loss and trying to figure out which direction to take their careers. Some are simply changing fields all together; shifting from finance to health care.

For many people, the disasters in this country also brought on joblessness; and there are more seniors in the work force trying to compete in the tighter job market against younger adults.

And don't forget the college graduates; they need to know where they fit in this equation. There's also been a rising need for teachers in our education system in this country.

So the demand for certain types of books has risen in some areas and decreased in others.

This doesn't mean that people aren't still reading novels, because they are; but there's an opening in the market for books on various topics.

When you self-publish, you can choose to meet the needs of a changing market at any time you please. If you see changes in your community that need to be addressed, then it's an opportunity for you to certainly pick up on that.

For instance, in the wake of all the changes going on in society, many folks have not addressed how these alterations have affected the black community. Similarly in times of universal struggle, African-Americans have been known to continuously have our needs neglected by the mainstream and therefore, it's difficult for us to find books that address what we are concerned about.

There have been several books written about American families who are faced with the reality of having to raise their households on less money, because they have lost their jobs, or about the many women have become single parents and widows due to unforeseen circumstances. But the affect on the African-American community at-large has not been addressed, and has in fact, been grossly overlooked. Who will tell our story?

Self-publishing is an outlet for the total expression that is sometimes needed in order to keep African-American informed.

Something to Think About

It's much easier for you, as a self-published author, to print things that the public needs without having to go through your agent, editor and publisher.

Now that the industry is aware that us black folk read, and read heavily, it is up to us to distribute the information that is well needed.

Writing for Artistic Integrity

Just like writing for creativity, you may want to write to tell the truth. In other words, sometimes when you get published and you get writing, your words may get changed. It's been my experience that some writers complain when they read the final edited version of their work and they find that the words are totally different.

What happens is an editor can adapt your words in the way they see fit. The problem with that is that this can change the meaning of your words and what you originally intended to say. It is your editor's job to edit but if you don't like what is written, then it's up to you to have that changed. But, most often you have to go with what the editor sees as being plausible in your work.

If you're like most writers, you don't want your meaning and intention changed from what you wanted it to be. Self-publishing, again, is the way you may want to go. The following writer had a similar experience in a conversation we had when I had altered one of his articles for the magazine.

> *James B.: I wasn't happy with the way you changed my words around. I didn't want my article to talk about how to please a woman but how a woman should please a man. I just wanted to let women know something they may not have known on what really pleases men in bed. It doesn't even sound like the same article I remember writing. The whole meaning of my article is lost now because of the changes you made.*

He had a valid point. I didn't intend to change the meaning of his work. But for space purposes, I had to cut down his article for that particular issue and there wasn't enough room to contain all that he wanted me to. So I had no other choice but to cut down his original manuscript.

If you don't want your work compromised because of space or anything else, then you should strongly consider self-publishing.

Take Control

There's nothing wrong with wanting to be in control of the way you handle your business. After all, it's your work! You should have the most control in putting it out that you can have.

African-American writers commonly come up against this obstacle, not only in writing, but outside of the industry as well.

We have been known to be stripped of our control in a variety of fields and situations. For those of us who fall into a lesser economic divide, it's even harder to gain control of the things around us. Sometimes life, quite frankly, feels like it's falling apart at the seams.

You can get back your control and publish something you can look at with pride; and there's nothing wrong with wanting that.

The Pride Factor

You want to publish a book that you can be proud of. For many writers, it's not a point of monetary value, but a point of having something in their lives to show for themselves. Writing is a difficult project, at times. It takes perseverance to push through the writer's blocks, rejections and disbelief you suffer through during the process.

It may not always be easy to get through what you're experiencing. Sometimes it seems like you'll never finish a project or get to see your work in print. I've personally struggled with that for most of my writing career. There were times when I actually put my pen down, stopped typing and swore to never write again.

But I couldn't shake the need to communicate truth and to get things out in the open, so I managed to get myself together and started to write anything...a short piece in the morning and something small everyday after that. It was better than writing nothing at all.

You might find this of some comfort to you. When it's all said and done and all the hard work is through, you'll have a product to look at with pride...excluding the fact of gaining some large sum of money, or getting a spot on Oprah. Your book is a reflection of you and your beliefs.

Hopefully, if you choose to self-publish, the words that you'll release will be inspiring and words that we all need.

It's Plain and Simple

If you pretty much like to be in control of what you do, then you should definitely self-publish. If you don't like dealing with someone telling you where, what and how, then don't run to a mainstream publisher, you'll only be more frustrated and can run into attitude problems when you want to do what it is you want.

When you want something,
you have to be willing to pay your dues.
—Les Brown

Chapter 2
So...How Shall I Define "Self-Publishing"?

You've read all the pros and cons of trying to get your book or articles published. However, you have a book of poems or a novel that you know will be a guaranteed bestseller. But publishing with a major house just doesn't sound appealing to you right now. You want to have complete creative control, being able to say what you want, write your own grammar and language, and eliminate the middleman; so you've decided that you're going to have to do it yourself.

Like the old adage says, 'if you want something done right, you have to do it yourself.' This is the best way to ensure the most control over your work and your visions, as you see fit. The greatest part about it is that you are the one who dictates how you want everything to be laid out.

Taking the step to self-publish gives you full creative control. You determine the typeset and the cover design. If you're also an artist, you get the freedom of designing whatever image appears on the cover. Sounds great, of course. And what's more important is, that you get to keep the profit. Yes, You get to keep 100% of all your earnings. There are no agents and no attorneys to profit off of you.

As more and more writers consider self-publishing, new methods become more accessible and easier to afford. And, when people speak of Self-Publishing, there is often confusion about the method that they are planning to use. In my attempt to bring clarity to the

11

subject, these are some of the things to consider about Traditional Publishers, Subsidy Publishers, Vanity Presses, Conventional Self-Publishing, Personalized Self-Publishing, On-Demand-Publishing—In other words, what's the difference?

▼ **A traditional publisher** purchases a manuscript as a property, and pays the author a royalty on sales (most also pay an advance on royalties). Royalty publishers screen submissions for quality, and handle every aspect of editing, publication, distribution, and marketing. There are no costs to the author.

▼ **A vanity publisher** (sometimes called a book producer) prints and binds a book at the author's sole expense. Costs include the publisher's profit and overhead, so vanity publishing is usually a good deal more expensive than self-publishing. (A typical print run is 1000 books @ $10 / $10,000). The completed books are the property of the author, and the author retains all proceeds from sales. Vanity publishers do not screen for quality—they publish anyone who can pay—and provide no editing, marketing, warehousing, or promotional services.

▼ **A subsidy publisher** (a.k.a. a joint venture publisher, a co-op publisher, a partner publisher, and many others) also takes payment from the author to print and bind a book, but may itself contribute a portion of the cost, as well as adjunct services such as editing, distribution, warehousing, and some degree of marketing. There may be some limited screening of submissions to rule out pornography or hate literature, but as with vanity publishers it's the author's cash, not the quality of his/her work, that counts. However, even though the author pays for the printing, the completed books are the property of the publisher (as with a royalty publisher) and remain in the publisher's possession until sold. Income to the writer comes in the form of a royalty, which may be paid every three to six months.

▼ **Conventional Self-publishing**, like vanity publishing, requires the author to undertake the entire cost of publication him/herself, and to handle all marketing, distribution, storage, etc. However, because the author can put each and every aspect of the process out to bid, rather than accepting a pre-set package of services, self-publishing can be much more cost-effective than vanity or subsidy publishing, and can result in a much higher-quality product. And unlike subsidy publishing, the completed books are the writer's property, and the writer keeps 100% of sales proceeds.

▼ **Personalized Self-publishing,** is a method of self-publishing that puts you in the hands of a personal consultant or guide. As with the Conventional Self-publishing method, the author is required to pay the entire cost of publication plus a minimal consultant fee to the Company. (This plan can actually save you money because you will be working with professionals who have already established industry relationships and have determined the best and most reputable designers and printers to work with). In turn, the company will confer with you about every step of the process needed to bring your manuscript to completion as a published book. They will advise you, but you make the final decisions. They will coordinate the entire project, edit your book, find the best prices, order the ISBN and the barcode, handle the design, production, printing and shipping details. You will retain all rights to your book and you keep 100 percent of each book sale.

▼ **Print-on-demand** is another option to consider. It's one of the fee-based companies that offers a service, which is a cross between vanity publishing and self-publishing. Usually, there are three different services offered—you will be given certain specs, colors, layouts and designs to choose from for both the cover and interior. You'll be able to select the look you prefer, but if you want to submit your own design you can—for extra money. This service is typically for paperbacks at a cost of around $700-$2000, which gives you 10 to 50 books. Once you pay for the service, the P.O.D. company will handle your distribution to the distributors, wholesalers and even some bookstores. They first deduct the cost per total book order and pay you a royalty check (about 10%-40%) every 3 months.

▼ **Ebook Publishing** is completely electronic. Your electronic book will be sold online on a designated website, maybe even yours. It would be set up so that the text could not be copied or printed, only read online after it is paid for. The major costs incurred come from setting up the files professionally in PDF format for online reading. You need a specific program and there are some publishing companies (print-on-demand) that offer this service, as well. On your website, of course, you would keep 100% of all sales; if you sell your ebook on someone else's website, you work out an arrangement for a certain percentage. To do business on-line, you also need to have a merchant account that would handle credit card sales.

Now that you know the differences, carefully consider the pros and cons and measure the advantages of the various routes you can take in your journey to fulfill your publishing goal.

In the meantime, in your quest to "self-publish" your book, consider these words of wisdom:

Limitations
Almost everything has its limitations, and as long as you keep within the guidelines of decency and do not infringe upon another group's rights through racist or pornographic depictions, then you are going to get your point across.

How Do You Get Paid?

Your payment cycle and amount depends on which type of program you're involved in.

Bear in mind, that in any royalty situation "proceeds" will always be less per book if you sell to a wholesaler, distributor or bookstore. The only sales that will probably pay the full price are "retail" sales.

If you self-publish your book, whether or not you are working with a company that manages the process for you or using a vanity press, you get paid 100% of the proceeds directly from the wholesaler, distributor, bookstore or retail customer.

With a "Print On demand", you get paid pre-determined royalties (10% - 40%) on your books sold in the same way as if you would have gone to a traditional or major publisher. The proceeds are sent to you, usually every three months, from every book sale

Ebook or online publishing pays on a per sale basis via credit card (into your merchant account). Unless you have other commission arrangements with a web-host or online bookstore, you keep 100% of the proceeds.

When do You Get Paid?

In many instances, you will be asked to send your books on consignment. Not only will you have to entrust books, but you will have to advance the cash for shipping. (Make sure you add shipping to your bill, when it's appropriate).

Always know the pay cycle of every client you sell books to. For instance, large wholesalers like Ingram and Baker & Taylor take the biggest discount and don't pay you until 90 days after they receive their books. Bookstores and libraries usually pay net 30; but you may be able to (depending on their policy) get a pre-paid purchase order.

In fact, it might be best to ask for prepayment as often as you can, since you are just starting your business and can't really afford to have too many books out with no immediate cash flow.

If you are doing business with an ODP make sure you know what the exact royalty payment cycle is, since you will have already laid out hundreds, if not, thousands of dollars to have them prepare your books.

In any event, set up a merchant account with your bank as soon as possible so you can take credit card sales. Being credit card ready will speed up your payment process and promote higher sales.

It's Plain & Simple

No matter which method of "self-publishing" you choose, I would suggest saving up at least twenty-five hundred to five thousand dollars, depending on the plan you choose. This gives you enough to pay for the initial cost of printing, shipping, and actually designing the book.

If you don't believe in yourself, then who will believe in you? The next man's way of getting there might not necessarily work for me, so I have to create my own ways of getting there.
—Martin Lawrence

Chapter 3
Getting the Word Out

Pros and Cons

The good thing about self-publishing is that, in the long run, you can always be picked up by a major publisher, or your book can simply gain success on its own, such as Teri Woods' book *True To The Game*. Her gritty and edgy dialogue have linked her with comparisons to the late Donald Goines.

Through word of mouth or the sheer marketing of your work, you could find that your book sells major, and suddenly, all eyes are on you. Everyone starts to await your next book. As a matter of fact, you're already in your second re-print and you can't seem to keep enough books in stock. With a following like this, you would be, undoubtedly, picked up by a major publisher, and hopefully given the big deal that all writers fantasize about.

Something To Think About

Once a major publisher accepts your book, all the leg-work will be out of your hands, and that means that not only would you be apt to get a great deal, but you've also bypassed any middle-man and can move forward to bigger and better things.

Once you are picked up by a major book publisher, you'll have more time to focus on your writing and less on trying to juggle being a businessperson and publisher.

Marketing

Perhaps the biggest task with self-publishing is the marketing aspect. Consider this. When you are signed to a Warner Books, Doubleday, Random House, etc. there will an entire department devoted to marketing your book through the Internet, TV, radio and magazines.

But, most self-publishing companies do not have the time to do such things. The most they can do is offer a brief description or advertising on their site. Other than that, the rest is up to you.

You see, once they print it and pay for those costs, your book is in print. They've done their part of the work; the rest is entirely up to you. So, if you want your book to be sold, the main thing you have to do is promote it. You must do all the legwork.

Call the bookstores and send them a review copy. Then schedule book signings and readings at your local bookstores. You also have to write to the magazines, newspapers and newsletters with a description of your book, as well as a sample copy. You should make sure you include a bio, as well.

Sometimes the bookstores will be interested; sometimes they won't be. But, this is perhaps the biggest risk; and this is where you must allocate enough time. If you're working full-time, making this a part-time job is the most convenient thing to do.

Be Thorough

Take the self-publishing route, only if you are willing to accept all the "extras" that are going to come along with it. Some writers cannot be bothered, others like having total control over everything that happens.

A Brief About Newspapers

Newspapers are probably the greatest way to gain local publicity, especially, if you have little or no experience, or name recognition.

Most local papers in your community have an editorial section, and they will help you voice your opinions about things that matter to you. It is typically non-paying, but you can benefit from being heard. Topics could range from abortion, to civil rights, to police brutality, and terrorism. And, your opinions are welcome.

Basic Tips

Pick up or subscribe to your local paper and write down the contact information. Which newspapers you choose to pitch is, of course, entirely your decision. I feel that it is best to approach African-American newspapers, newsletters and journals that cross a broad spectrum from political topics to entertainment.

Local newspapers touch upon a number of issues relating to Caribbean and African cultures; and with this vast pool of information, it's very difficult not to find somewhere to write, vent, get tension off your chest, or just speak out. As an author, getting your name in the paper and your voice heard as often as possible is your ultimate goal.

Internet Publishing

To some, Internet Publishing is considered the new way of the future. This is a perfect, easily accessible way to get published and have your voice heard. If you're reading this book, you are looking to get your words in print, but don't know where to start.

Your poetry and stories are good, but where you can go with seeing your words on the Internet, can make you available to literally millions of people who surf the web everyday. There is no pay in such expressions unless you are actually on staff at the particular website or choose to charge a fee for each time viewers log in. But, what a fast way to get your word out it! There are more forums online than you can even count.

You can also find a listing of sites where writers can convene and discuss topics all across the board. You can get the most out of networking at these sites while getting helpful tips and information.

It's Plain & Simple

What seems to be an incredible amount of work should also be a labor of love to you. It can make you more involved with the work you're putting out. This ends up being a full-time job, no matter how you look at it.

It doesn't matter how many say it cannot be done or how many people have tried it before; it's important to realize that whatever you're doing, it's your first attempt at it.
—Wally Amos

Chapter 4
Managing Your Writing Career

If you plan to self-publish, you can do so by approaching it like any business-person would when starting a business.

First, you have to do the background leg-work, that is, formulating it as if you were opening up a store. Now you may not choose to have a complete publishing company where you actually publish other works, but being organized in this way is going to help you put out your book with a definite plan and purpose.

You don't have to be an accountant or a financial planner; just follow the simple plans and you'll be done with what is perhaps the most time consuming part of self-publishing.

The Business Plan

You know what business you're in. So ask yourself the next questions. What are your products? Services? And what is your target market? If you're going to put out a book targeted to young African-American teens, you should know your market first.

The body of your self-publishing business can be divided into four sections:

(1) The description of your business
(2) Your marketing plan

(3) Your financial plan

(4) Your management plan, for how you'll handle it once the book is done and out on the market.

If you are planning to open up a business, which will publish other works, then you have to also include supporting documents, an executive summary and financial (future) projects.

Follow the example(s) below and fill it in to match your specific plan. It will help you follow the flow and keep track of all the money that you spend and get in from the sales of your book.

You need your Business Plan first. In your business plan, you have to break down, and be specific about the following:

▼ Your Business Description—what is your mission and what type of book(s) will you offer

▼ Marketing Plan—how will you sell the book(s)

▼ Financial plan—include any loan applications, equipment and supply lists, and a balance sheet , where you keep track of how much you earn and how much you put back into printing more copies.

All of this information is beneficial, especially when it comes down to tax time.

One of the most difficult decisions to make is what price? How much should you sell your book for, so that others don't think it's too much to pay? Is your price competitive, below or above the competition?

Get a feel for the prices of similar books on the market. If you are publishing a book about cosmetology, try to keep your book priced about the same or lower than what is out there.

You could price above the competition, however, if your book contains more information than the existing books on the market.

In your business plan, you should add in the cost of materials (if any) as well as your labor costs. Be honest about how much you're making and reinvesting in the business. It's important to staying above water in this business.

Make sure that your prices cover your production costs and leaves a big enough margin for profit. That is, make sure you're not spending more than you're making back. In your opinion, is the price suggested to you by the printing company too steep?

Your initial start-up budget should consist of any personnel or assistants you pay, any legal fees, printing/computer equipment, business insurance, office supplies, advertising/promotions, income, utilities, design and printing costs, and any number of additional miscellaneous expenses.

Think About An Income Statement

This is what you're projecting in terms of profit when you've begun selling your books. It primarily consists of your:

- ▼ Total net sales
- ▼ Cost of your book sales
- ▼ Gross profit
- ▼ Gross profit margin

All of these are optional when thinking about writing the business plan.

The income statement or profit and loss statement, as it's called, is a tool to help control your business operations; that is, your input versus your output. Its main purpose is to give you an estimate of the amount of monthly sales, as well as your expenses.

Analyze Your Market

▼ Who are the customers/readers of your books?

▼ What is the competition out there? Who is selling the same type of book you're marketing?

▼ Do books like yours do generally well or not so well? If your book is about fixing cars, then you'll be popular primarily amongst mechanics or car lovers. You should have realistic expectations of what your book is going to make. Don't fall into the trap of getting discouraged because your first book doesn't do very well. There's always a next time.

If you're fronting the business yourself, you have to be especially careful with your money.

Ask Yourself:

1. How much money do you have?

2. How much money are you willing to spend?

3. How much money will you need to stay in business after your first book comes out?

You are a business. Keeping organized is going to ensure your longevity. Maintain files of all the books you've sold as well as all your expenses. Although you're primarily in the business of only publishing your own book, files will help you keep track of your funds.

You don't need to have a staff, office space, or a number of investors to be considered a business entity. Once you publish a manuscript, you are going to sell that work and that makes those transactions a business.

Reinvest Wisely

To make sure you don't exceed your budget, create a sound financial plan by determining the amount of money needed to initially print your books and the amount needed to reprint.

Write down how many months/years you've been in business for yourself, your initial price of the book, and mark down how competitive the market is. You can range this as very much, little, etc. or high, medium or low competition.

Remember this is just a brief overview. If you need in-depth information you should go to a number of financial books that are on the market. If you are serious, then you should get the detailed information you need.

Self Check

Now follow these simple tips toward a successful Self-Publishing Career:

▼ List the health of your industry.

▼ Is your style of book popular and in demand right now?

▼ Look at economic trends also. Are people buying books like yours now or are they looking for self-help guides?

▼ List what you're strong in. If financial matters are not your thing, then you should enlist the help of a relative who is good with money. Does spell checking or checking for grammatical errors leave you stumped? Get help from that English major in your family or down the street from you.

▼ How is your book better than the competition? Is your novel racier? Is your book addressing an issue in your community that most other writers are scared to address?

▼ How is your book lacking from others on the market? Are there a number of details you're leaving out? Is there something important you should have addressed, say about hairdressing, which you didn't? What are ways for you to make your book stronger?

▼ Where will you get your printing supplies if you're not going to get your book done professionally somewhere else?

List as many considerations here as you need.

Now select the forms of marketing that you are going to be using, because you may not have the money or the time to use all the means open to you.

▼ Television_____

▼ Radio_____

▼ Newspapers_____

▼ Local Bookstores_____

▼ Direct Mail_____

▼ Personal (Word Of Mouth)_____

▼ Magazines_____

Whatever form you choose, just make sure your supply meets your demand, and that you're spending within your budget. It may be hard on you if you give yourself a short time to increase production. It's all up to you. You should desire to be unique, and strike people's curiosity, making them want to choose your book over others. With thorough research and time you can do this.

It's Plain & Simple

Always consult a financial consultant or professional if you're confused about what to do in terms of your business planning. It doesn't hurt to know a little about how your business operates so after you've sold a trunk load of books, you're not left wondering what happened with your money.

Get your ideas on paper and study them.
Do not let them go to waste!
—Les Brown

Chapter 5
Creating Your Ideas

This is where the writing process starts.

Many writers submit works to magazines and publishers and have not specifically indicated what they really wanted to get across. Know your audience and what they're looking for, and be specific. For example, if you are writing an article to target a children's market, you have to make sure to refrain from using hard language or words that may be too complicated.

Use the following suggestions in order to get you properly on the right track:

▼ Ideas are formatted through a serious thought process. There are concrete ways to note this for future reference.

▼ No one can pinpoint your ideas for you.

▼ The key factor is to make sure you have a crystal clear idea of what it is you want to say.

Nothing is worse than having an idea and not quite knowing how to put it down. If that happens, you'll have a manuscript that is difficult to understand. This was the case of one well-known mainstream writer. Her first novel gathered a substantial following but when she worked on her second and third books, they were very confusing and she lost many fans. Jumping from one idea to another without thoroughly explaining one idea first, can to result in a book that warms bookshelves but not people.

We all work differently. Many of us can't keep all our ideas in our heads; so writing out an outline first would actually be a good way to start. Our outlines may vary, of course. But they are good tools for those like myself, who can't remember all the ideas gathered in our heads.

For Example:

This example can help you organize your ideas. It applies to someone who wants to write a book about ending a relationship smoothly:

Outline
1. How To Break Up
   a. When to leave a bad relationship
   b. Ways to tell your lover
2. Accepting the reaction
   a. When counseling is needed
   b. Moving on
   c. Beginning life by yourself
3. Seeking Outside Counseling
4. Conclusion

Write it down

Trying to keep a clutter of information in your head solely, is not going to work in most cases. This is simple and self-explanatory. Writing down all of your ideas is the best way to make sure you are concise. And try to write things meticulously, in a way that you'll understand when you go back to review your notes. Better yet, whenever possible, you'll find that it's more practical in the long run to input your ideas directly into your computer.

Since this is the starting point of every manuscript, it should be considered as the most important step. After getting your ideas together, sort them out by time or in a specific sequence so that you're not skipping back and forth, starting at the end and then going back to the beginning.

Research

If you're writing about how to buy an antique car, for example, make sure you know all there is to know. The Internet provides all of, or at least much of the information you'll need. Visit the library for additional information on the subject. If you vaguely know what you're talking about, it's going to affect your finished product and diminish your potential as an established author. Readers can quickly tell when you don't know your subject.

If you want to test the waters first before you go the route of self-publishing, submit a short-story to a magazine editor; but, make sure you know exactly what you're talking about. Incorrectly stating your facts will immediately get your article rejected, even if it is well written. So before you send anything anywhere, research, research, research.

Being vague or incorrect shows a sloppy writer that no one will want to work with. As a magazine editor, I receive many story submissions. Once I had a writer submit an article to me about men who were sociopaths. However, she incorrectly stated that almost every man with a tattoo is a sociopath. Well, I, as well as many others, have known plenty of African-American men with tattoos who weren't sociopaths. Needless to say, the story was rejected.

Rough draft it

Once you've gotten your notes and have done your research, it's time to get it all down. At this stage, there's no need to make it perfect. As a matter of fact, the key to making a good rough draft is to keep it as informal as possible.

Many writers shy away from the rough draft, opting instead, to begin on the final copy right after they've gotten their notes together. But, I recommend giving yourself enough time to put your notes together in a format that will make your writing more coherent and precise. Working in this manner can be beneficial because you can go over the rough draft before you complete your manuscript to make sure that what you have written is accurate.

Stay the Course

Remember, writing is not an easy process. Sometimes it could take years just to complete one novel. Many writers get over-anxious early in their careers because they expect to spit out a book in record time without really concentrating on the little details.

Consider that one chapter can go through a number of drafts; so if you imagine you have a work with thirty chapters…that's twenty-nine more drafts you'll have to go through. But, in the long run it will be well worth it.

So write the first thoughts that come to your head. They aren't engraved in stone and don't have to remain the way you first put them down. Once you've done that, simply go back and perfect what you started. I can guarantee when you've read through it a second time, you'll find errors and discrepancies that you hadn't noticed the first time around. It's good practice to start this way and keep it up.

Watch Your Language

Most importantly, make sure you use the right words. I have come across many writers who submit editorials to magazines; and they have no idea what they're talking about. Using large words does not make you a more prolific writer. As a matter of fact, it can make you sound foolish.

The best rule is to stick with what you know. If you're using a word and you don't fully understand what it means, don't use it. This can be a clear path toward having your work rejected by a publisher or editor, even if you've spent hours putting it together.

I once received a manuscript from a writer who used so many words she didn't understand, that I almost felt embarrassed for her. I couldn't believe this woman claimed to have been published in large magazines when it was clear she had not only a comprehension problem, but a spelling problem as well.

If you're ever in doubt, it might be best to have your manuscript reviewed by someone who is good in spelling and grammar. If you happen to be a student, you can ask the advice of an English teacher, counselor or classmate who is an English major.

Take Your Time

A manuscript can never be too perfect to you. You are the writer and if you go over a piece a thousand times, there will always be something wrong with it. You're job is to make it as good as you can. Before you publish your book, make sure you ask someone who is not associated with it to edit the manuscript.

This, however, should never be an excuse to make your work sloppy. Taking your time ensures that you have made the conscious effort to assure that it is appropriate and concise. So many writers get trapped in this race for time that they end up getting surprised when their work is criticized or rejected.

Something To Think About:

If you're one of those writers who is lucky enough to create a masterpiece in a matter of minutes, then go for it. But, if you're trying to write for money, and that is your sole purpose, then it is especially important that you take your time. The slightest grammatical error can leave your manuscript unchecked and promptly returned to you.

Watch Your Tense

As the editor of *Jive/Intimacy* Black romance magazines, I specifically noticed this in countless manuscripts. At the magazine, we had required that all stories should be written in past tense. However, many writers would constantly switch from past to present tense. When editors see this type of behavior, they may believe that you have forgotten what you previously wrote. And, in their eyes, it usually reveals a writer that needs much more training. To be successful as an author, you must keep everything in order. That's why taking your time is so important; you may be able to catch these seemingly little mistakes.

These have been examples of how to gather your ideas before formatting your final manuscript. The final work should be as concise and clear as possible. The main thing to keep in mind is something I learned in high school.

When writing an article, you should always remember that you are speaking to your readers as if they have no knowledge at all of what you're talking about. For example, there are plenty of people who know of popular hip-hop groups and singers such as R. Kelly. And yet, if you were to write a book about the popular singer, you would have to slant your piece to the public as if they'd never heard of him, before giving a brief history of his career, and then proceeding with the interview or whatever information you choose to detail.

But besides focusing on the subject, you must remember not to switch tenses. If you began your paragraph in the present, stay there unless it's crucial to show some type of flashback in your story. And, once again, if you're unsure, just run your manuscript past someone who you think will be helpful. Any reputable editor would recommend it.

Formatting Your Ideas Further

Actually, this is the hardest part of the writing process. Some writers are fortunate to be able to sit down and weave tales without having to have a synopsis or format. But, for most of us, it's good to have our ideas ready before we sit down and begin to write.

Be Thorough

There are a number of questions to ask yourself during character development.

▼ The age of the character(s)?

▼ Physical characteristics?

▼ Their likes and dislikes?

▼ Where were they born?

▼ Any kids?

▼ Sexual orientation?

Character development is crucial to constructing a story that makes sense and engulfs readers. Where is the story set? Where are the characters from? What are the characters' favorite colors? What are the characters' favorite places to travel?

It's important to make these characters as believable as possible. This way you can make the reader follow and relate to the story. Essentially, that is what is going to sell even if the characters are highly unlike the readers.

For example, the series of books by the late Donald Goines were focused on characters, like Iceburg Slim who were from the ghetto. The writing style was urban and gritty. Even if the readers are completely different from them, they will still relate based upon how real and honest the characters are.

Understand Writer's Block

If you're reading this book, you probably love to write and you know that sometimes it can be a difficult task. There will be times when you can sit and stare at a piece of paper forever and will not be able to come up with anything. No words will come…possibly for a long time…days…weeks…even months. During this time, you may become frustrated; but, be patient, words will come when they need to.

The bottom line is—if you don't have a single, concrete idea, then you've already been defeated before you begin. And there is probably no easier way to start than just taking some time away from your computer or getting some rest. Or, sometimes, you might just need to go to the gym to work out. Writer's block doesn't last forever; it comes and goes. That's the real nature of it.

In the meantime, rather than getting frustrated or upset, learn to respect it and step away.

Most often, if you're plagued by writer's block, it's because you've spent too much time writing or thinking and trying to get things out of your head. All that pressure you're putting on yourself is bound to result in burnout.

Once those ideas start to flow, everything is going to come to you. Always be ready to begin, and when the ideas begin to flow, keep in mind the following suggestions:

▼ Write it down
▼ Do your research
▼ Rough draft it
▼ Watch your language
▼ Take your time
▼ Watch your tense
▼ Understand writer's block

So, don't fight against it. Just go with the flow and chill for a minute. The ideas will come back shortly if you give yourself a break.

It's Plain & Simple

Every finished book begins with an idea. It also ties in with knowing exactly what you want to say and what voice you want to say it in.

*It's better to be prepared for an opportunity and not have
one than to have an opportunity and not be prepared.*
—Whitney Young, Jr.

Chapter 6
Fine Tuning Your Manuscript

Now that you've noted your ideas, you should be ready to format your final manuscript.

After you've made countless rewrites and are confident about what you have written, your manuscript should certainly meet your approval. But, there's more work to be done before you complete your final draft. Don't assume that once you have a presentable manuscript, the bulk of your work is done. Now, you must do the most crucial part—organize your manuscript.

Self Check

A great way to measure the acceptance of your work before you self-publish is to pitch your work to magazines. This will also help you to get more organized.

Many noted African-American authors have gained notoriety from national magazines prior to having their first book published. This process will help you create a "following" and, as a result, make your book easier to market. So quite naturally, you'll probably want to submit your manuscript to one of the many African-American magazines where you will stand a chance of having an excerpt published.

Ebony, Essence, Black Enterprise, Heart & Soul magazine, and many, if not all African-American magazines see manuscripts daily, lots of them. So, it's up to you to prove to an editor or publisher that your manuscript is worth featuring. It may take some time for the magazine to contact you, but keep in mind that a poorly constructed manuscript will more than likely get rejected, even if it's well written.

The following basic tips can propel you from being merely "considered" to actually being "published":

Include your information

Contact Information	Usually, at the top left-hand corner of your manuscript, you'd list your name, address, phone number and e-mail address.
	This is a given for most manuscripts, and should be typed in a smaller font, if possible, but it is not important. Some writers actually forget to include their contact information.
Self-addressed Stamped Envelope (SASE)	And, I can never say this enough. If you want your manuscript returned to you, please submit a self-addressed stamped envelope. The publication cannot afford to take the time to make out an envelope for you. Time is money to them and they're not going to do it.
	If you don't submit a SASE, then don't expect your work to be returned to you.
Word Count	On the top right hand corner, it is best to list how many words the piece is. (i.e. 6,500 words, etc.)

Type It

Computers are everywhere. Most of us don't do anything without them. A simple pen and paper is basic and always good to have around, just in case, but handwriting anything is not professional and will simply get your work thrown away.

Be Thorough

Here are some presentation rules:

▼ Always format your work with one-inch margins and it must be double-spaced.

▼ Times Roman is the standard typestyle in a size-12 font.

▼ Include the page number, typed preferably at the bottom of every page.

▼ At the top of each page, your last name should be placed on the left and the title of the manuscript on the right as follows (but let the software do this in the "header" feature):

Glover/No Hands   1

If you have to use a typewriter because you don't have access to a computer, follow the same presentation rules—your work must always be typed double-spaced, with your information included on every page.

Neat and Precise

As an editor, I received manuscripts stained with coffee, cheese and some other stuff I couldn't describe. Please don't go eat anything while you're working; If you smudge it on your text, it just shows that you are disorganized. And it may be assumed that if you don't care enough to make sure your copy is clean, you may not care enough to follow up on your manuscript when you should. Under these circumstances, it is very likely that your work will end up in the trash.

All of this advice may sound trivial, but it slips up so many writers time after time. So when you're ready to write, set aside nothing but time to do that. And keep the food away from your copy.

Spelling

Your manuscript should be as tight as possible before submission. Please use the spell check, grab the dictionary, and do whatever you have to do to clean up those errors. This is another mishap. Spelling "typically" as "tipicelly" is just plain ridiculous. But, many aspiring writers do this and are in disbelief when their work gets rejected.

The editor is not responsible for clearing up your mistakes. There are too many writers and deadlines to meet for others to correct your spelling.

Watch the grammar

"We is" and "What we be doing" don't cut it for any publication. Too often, African-American writers, may strike a cord with "ebonics" and believe that simply because the publication is African-American, that they accept slang language. But these magazines are like any other mainstream magazine…they don't make exceptions when it comes to proper English.

Remember, your audience will be from many different backgrounds. The sister in the hood reads *Essence* just as the corporate sister on Wall Street who makes big money for her clients. Sometimes certain slang is cool like 'sista' or 'brotha', but just make sure it doesn't sound cliché and has a definite purpose in adding to the article's content.

Other grammatical errors are not as blatant. For example, writing "We are must that to happen." This sentence obviously makes no sense. But what has happened is the writer confused what they were going to say and it all ended up coming out like a jumbled mess of nothing. Even one grammatical error can prevent your voice from being heard.

Something To Think About

You want your work to reach as many people as possible, so to be on the safe side, just keep the language basic. Don't belittle your readers by making the mistake of assuming the brother or sister in the ghetto doesn't understand common language. All that will be is the pot calling the kettle black; and that is precisely how predominantly white publishers victimized African-Americans for years.

So, to recap, if you want to gain notoriety through magazines you must be careful to not load your work with "ebonics". If you "self-publish" your work, however, it's your prerogative.

The Body of a Manuscript

There are three things to note…everything has *a beginning, a middle,* and *an ending.*

It is best to follow one concrete thought at a time; don't shift around when you are within paragraphs.

Introduce your topic. If you were trying to pitch an article about an up-and-coming singer, you'd want to include the basics like, where she is from, what type of music influenced her, and how she describes the most important collaborative efforts regarding her songs.

The following is an example of an introduction of your manuscript for submission to a magazine.

Jessica Somebody   *360 words*
555 West North Ave.
Akron, Ohio 00008
e-mail: 0;5555@nonews.com

Carlotta: Starlet Not Harlot
By Jessica Somebody

She's the coolest, sultry songstress to arrive in Atlanta, Georgia's budding hip-hop/pop culture. While her roots in the church may have given her the beginnings, her background, she insists, had music in her heart from birth.

"I sang and danced when I was two years old. I used to perform for daddy and mom's house guests." From this she was inspired to do many more things that she had only imagined…such is her debut album. The 22-year-old has penned her latest single on Macktress Records. She worked with the talented producers, Scoop C., Doobie, and Philly Moda, to name a few. It's no wonder her future is leading her in places beyond her wildest imagination.

Her tour this fall will show all the true talent she has, and proves that to whom much is given, much is expected.

It's Plain & Simple

Thousands of manuscripts are sent from writers all over the world, so you must always remember to make your manuscript stand out. This is important and the first consideration as to whether or not your story may get published in a magazine.

If you want to accomplish the goals of your life,
you have to begin with the Spirit.
—Oprah Winfrey

Chapter 7
Crafting Your Book

By now, you probably have a good idea what it takes to get your work published by a mainstream publisher. But, the road is a little more involved when you choose to self-publish, whereby you will be responsible for the entire publishing process from start to finish. That means getting the copyright, layout, binding and everything. This is the total construction of the book from head to toe. You will also be required to devote some time and attention to the inside acknowledgment, foreword, introduction and a photo as well as other things you might want to include. But, in the long run, you can have 100% control of the outcome.

The Final, Completed Manuscript

Saving your manuscript in Microsoft word and backing it up on a disk is a good idea, and it's safe for you. You'll need to have the manuscript stored somewhere. And if you don't have a computer, then it's best to go to someone who does have one and save your work on a disk. Besides it's just the smart thing to do. You may find yourself needing to make corrections on your work time and time again and you have to be able to refer to it somewhere.

Now you can adapt this manuscript to any number of desktop publishing programs that are available. One program that I used to self-publish my first poetry book was called Publisher 3. However, it was an older version and a bit difficult to understand at first.

Be Thorough

Visit your local business supply and/or computer store for a selection of programs. These are available on CD-ROM and are compatible usually to IBM and/or Mac systems unless otherwise specified.

It is easier if you locate a local desktop publisher who will take the text from your disk and format it into book form. Be sure to check your font style to ensure that the book has the look you want.

The Production Process

Since the overall production of your book is probably the most detailed work you'll have to do, the best way to gather the instructions you need to put your book together is to simply study the design of other books on the market.

We've already explored the cover design possibilities, which are open to your own interpretation, granted that it isn't too obscene. You don't want to produce a book that will be difficult to market over the mainstream.

Where binding, layout, and typeset copy are concerned, there are individuals or companies that can help you put this together for a fee. You won't have to worry about the formation of the book; and this is so much better than trying to put it together yourself at home. In this day and age, putting it together seems incredibly difficult and highly unethical.

Let's look at the basics of what your book will require—copy-editing, design, production and printing. One such company that provides complete service for your basic publishing needs to you as a *self-published* author is Quality Press. (details are listed in Appendix A). All you have to do is supply the manuscript and the fee.

Cover Design

If you're searching for ideas, you can research books that are currently on the market. Having a cover that is colorful and catchy may help in drawing attention to your book; and since what you want is sales, having this work for your marketing strategy is beneficial financially.

Using your own artistic skills can be convenient and cheap. Your publisher will then transfer the image to the cover.

You can have an artist draw a picture that best represents the book or you can place a photo on the cover. Add in a separate cost for the artist, however, if you are planning to use their work. With self-publishing, however you choose to do it, is entirely up to you, of course.

Copyright

I'd strongly advise you to get your work copyrighted. This should be done once your first draft is completed. Having this legal protection will keep you from being plagiarized and not being able to do anything about it.

You can get your work copyrighted by first getting all the necessary paperwork. The fee to copyright is $30.

To apply for registration, you may request all your information by writing to:

Library of Congress
Copyright Office
101 Independence Avenue, S.E.
Washington, D.C. 20559-6000

(When you inquire about information in writing it should come to you in 4-6 weeks).

To speed up the process, look online at http://lcweb.loc.gov/copyright for information and to download the necessary form (Form TX).

For further information on current fees, call the Copyright Public Information Office at (202) 707-3000, 8:30 a.m. to 5:00 p.m. eastern time, Monday through Friday, except federal holidays.

Upon receipt of your information, you'll notice that they require three things:

▼ A completed and signed application form.
▼ A $30.00 nonrefundable filing fee for each application, and;
▼ A non-returnable copy of the work to be registered.

Requested copyright announcements and circulars are available by fax, at 202-707-2600. You have to key in your fax number at the prompt and the document number of the item(s) you want to receive. The item(s) will be sent to your fax machine. But copyright application forms are not available by fax.

If you want an easier option and are Internet savvy, all U.S. Copyright application forms are available on the Internet. These can be downloaded and printed. Connect to the Library of Congress home page on the web and select the copyright link.

The address is: lcweb.loc.gov or http://lcweb.loc.gov/copyright. You must have Adobe® Acrobat® Readers installed on your computer to view and print the forms. The free program can be downloaded from the same copyright Internet site. If you need further information you can get all of that from this website or the information they mail to you.

It's Plain & Simple

If you're really serious about trying to get your work published, then you should set aside the money and invest in using a self-publishing provider.

Any writer, I suppose, feels that the world
into which he was born is nothing less than
a conspiracy against the cultivation of his talent.
—James Baldwin

Chapter 8
Gaining Editorial Exposure

You've digested a lot of information. Now that you've gotten your book into production, you might wish to submitted a few pieces to different magazines. Some will respond favorably...and some...not at all. Some may even begin to commission you to write for them.

Your writing career may be small at this point, but it has begun. You may soon have the privilege of looking in a magazine and seeing your name in print. You're writing is well on its way.

No doubt, rejection has been a common occurrence, as well. Even though you may have written what you consider to be a masterpiece, there will still be an editor who believes your work is not suitable for their publication. Do not get discouraged. Your work isn't going to please everyone all of the time.

But, if you follow my steps, soon you'll have to manage what you're going to do with the all money you have coming in.

If romance is your forte, make sure the magazine that you pitch is receptive to receiving articles that are romantic in nature. You wouldn't send a romance piece to hunting magazines. Never send your magazine to a publication that you have not studied; do the homework.

When I was editor of *Black Secrets,* a writer mailed me his manuscript to me about the black, dark practices of the under world occults.

However, *Black Secrets* is a black romance magazine. This man did not take the time to find that out. So he typed his article, put in a self-addressed stamped envelope, wasted his postage and mailed it to me. Needless to say, after I read the first line, I promptly returned it.

But You Don't Want to Purchase the Magazine

Well, this is hard for some folks. Let's face it, most magazines are not cheap, but the price you pay is nothing compared to the rewards of getting published.

However, you can review your market equally well if you purchase *The Writer's Market*, which is published by The Writer's Digest. And, if you prefer not to spend the money, you should be able to find it at the local library in the reference section. *The Writer's Market* is printed every year and details all of the magazines, large and small, throughout the country. It gives a thorough description of where to get your things published and what the publication is, as well as the pay rate and frequency of publication.

Surprisingly, you'll find that some publications will send you a free copy of their magazine, along with their publishing guidelines. It's worth checking out. And make sure you know the name of the current editor. You don't want the mail to get lost among faces in an office that are unfamiliar with the person you're trying to reach.

Read the Publication

This is a big part of the process. Sometimes your manuscript may stray from what is normally permitted in a magazine's format. This is why referring to the writer's guidelines makes sense. Using slang when the vernacular is especially academic, is a no-no. And if the manuscripts are normally written in second-person format, you shouldn't submit a confessional.

It shows that you haven't researched and you are not really interested in their publication. The following are a list of factors you must investigate before sending your hard-written work out to the public.

Payment

Some writers make assumptions right off. They assume that because one magazine pays $350.00 for an article that another magazine will pay them the same amount for the same article. Wrong! Every magazine has a different budget and criteria. Don't sit and harass the editors and assistants about why their pay is so low. If you believe your work is worth more money, you should calmly take the manuscript to a better paying magazine.

Do not try to get a publisher to change their rates for you because you don't think it's fair. A lot of things in life are not fair. And you should be adult enough to accept that which you cannot control.

In the past, I've gotten into little debates with writers because they felt like I should try to get them more money. It doesn't work that way; and an editor will tell you if you don't like it, to take it somewhere else.

I had been the struggling freelance writer, huffing to make deadlines around my nine to five, with the bills gathering all around me. At one point, I had two jobs; but the fact remained that I simply loved to write and knew that one day my patience would pay off. I believed that, with dedication, my dreams would eventually be realized and the real money would come when the time was right.

Be Thorough

Before you submit your work, you should investigate whether a publication pays on, before or after publication. The worst possible thing you can do is to concern editors regarding payment. I've encountered many writers who have depended upon their freelance checks to pay bills, mortgages and other essential expenses.

So often, writers get caught up in their own little world. The bills that they're going to pay when the next check comes in. You must sometimes understand, many black magazines are short-staffed;

unfortunately many editors handle not only editorial work but also the deadlines of payroll for writers as well. Keep this in mind when you are submitting your work to certain publications.

Do not send harassing letters or make phone calls that are so persistent everyone in the accounting department knows you by name. The professional way to get paid is to follow up by writing, and be specific. If the editor has already sent a contract to you, and literally months (three or more) have passed without getting paid, indicate on your fax or in your phone call, the issue, publication date, amount, and said article for which you have not received payment.

To Know the Staff

It pays to understand the publisher you're working with, and get to know more about the staff. What are they dealing with? Know to whom you're speaking and how you should address certain manuscripts. At larger magazines, such as *Black Enterprise,* there is a large enough staff to address specific queries and questions to direct department editors. Other magazines might just require you to address your package to "Editor".

Basic Tips:

▼ Don't make personal visits to the editorial office unless you are invited.

▼ Always be polite when you call for information.

▼ Do the research to find out how to address your package. *Don't address a relationship article to the health editor.*

You are in this industry for exposure; and this is the beginning of your path to becoming a great writer. Magazines always need writers—good writers. There are people out there looking for you all the time. The magazine that publishes your work will help you gain the exposure you need to step up into the winners' circle of well-known authors. So get your pen ready, use professionalism.

Ask About Publication Times

Do not expect your magazine article to be out on the newsstands right away. I had a friend who wrote for many genres, including sports. After submitting a piece to a mainstream magazine, the editor was interested.

However, weeks had passed and the editor didn't have the time to promptly get back to the writer. So, the writer persisted to call over and over again, until the editor finally felt pressured to discuss her work with her.

If the writer had studied more closely, what the publication dates were, she wouldn't have hounded the editor. In other words, some publications take two to three months to respond; others take six months to respond to your query or submission. Be patient and don't call the office before the date specified.

How do you know what their time line is? This goes back to studying the magazine. If they say it will take eight months to respond to your query, don't call them after three months and expect them to give you a response. And if you don't know the time, send a self-addressed stamped envelope with an index card inside, asking them to tell you what the response time is.

> ## Something To Think About
>
> If an editor feels pressured by you because you're calling too much or being too persistent, you may be viewed as a trouble-maker and your work could get rejected immediately. Unfortunately, so many writers make this mistake. Follow-up, of course, but don't be a pest.

Use the Mail

Sending a postcard, or even e-mail, if it's available to you, is the best way to confirm whether your manuscript has been received.

If you call, you'll probably spend time speaking to an answering machine. And you may not even get a call back for some weeks or even months. A lot of editors don't have much time to get back to the numerous phone calls they receive.

Use The Fax

If you have any questions, you can also direct them by fax. I had a writer call me inquiring about payment. She had already called the accounting department with her questions; and they in turn, forwarded her questions to me.

It is not professional to bother staff in other departments if you are inquiring about response time or payment. Unprofessional or demanding writers may also be placed on a restricted list as you'll read about next.

The Restricted List

Every editor has this list, which you should avoid, at all costs. It includes writers who are overly aggressive, abusive, plagiarists or unprofessional, and who become a nuisance to the point that none of their work can be considered. In fact, if you are too persistent, legal action can be taken against you if you are considered being harassing or threatening.

You may be of no physical threat, but editors don't have time to tailor their work specifically to you alone.

Circulation

It may be of some interest for you to find out the circulation of the magazine you are pitching. If you'd like to personally know how many people you are bound to reach, this is helpful information.

Subject Matter

This relates directly to the previous point. Make sure your subject matter speaks to your intended audience. It is best to target your words accordingly. Take your time, and do as many drafts as you need to make the article acceptable for the particular publication.

Focus is key. Without this, your article is doomed for failure. So making sure that you're speaking on a topic that will be of interest to the magazine's audience is the degree of quality you put into your career as a writer. This is key to getting your audience to fully relate to the message you are trying to convey.

Understand "The Rights"

This is extremely important. Magazines and publications can buy first rights, all rights, or a varying degree of both.

If a publication wants to buy all rights to your work, it means they own it upon your writing it for them. If they buy first rights, it means they only have the rights at the time of publication, which after the magazine goes off newsstands, you retain the rights.

All rights are usually agreeable to most writers; but when a publication buys all rights, it means you can't later submit it to another magazine because it becomes the property of the publication. If you're writing a short story and are so loaded with stories that you don't mind selling your work for all rights, that's fine. If you're work is just that good to you and you want to later send it elsewhere for consideration, then you wouldn't want to give all rights to anyone.

This is very important because you usually sign a contract when you work with a magazine and you don't want to go against your contract. After you've pinpointed publications that you like, be sure to ask them what rights they require. It will save you a lot of trouble in the long run. You don't want to give up the rights for a work you truly wanted to keep legally. I personally think this is the first question you should ask a publication when dealing with them.

Time Matters

Now that your work has been accepted by a magazine, this is probably going to be the most crucial part of your planning. As your work increases, you'll notice that you have to schedule time for meeting deadlines.

Self Check

Give yourself the necessary room for research. Having interviews is especially important if you're writing something heavily relying upon facts. If you work a nine-to-five job or more than one job, this can be very critical. And, scheduling one article at the beginning of the week, and a second article at the end, may be too much to handle. So, be sure to pace yourself.

Build Your Portfolio Gradually

Exciting is the word to describe this. Remember, in the beginning you thought a writing career was the farthest from your reach; but now that you are on top, you're getting your work in more and more magazines. Friends, colleagues and family members can open up the pages of magazines and see your name as the author.

It is important to safely store you finished magazines or tear sheets, as they're called, in a binder of some sort. This illustrates your work, if you want to increase your work experience, and your ability to get freelance writing assignments.

Full-Time Freelance Writing

It is possible, for the writer who is awaiting publication of their book or a staff position at a magazine, to make a consistent living writing for numerous magazines. If your writing is favorable, you could manage to get a contributing writer label and manage to secure constant jobs.

I had a similar experience with my work when I was editor at one magazine. A fellow co-worker whom I had worked with at a previous publication had just landed a new job.

In a crunch, one of her writers had neglected to deliver a piece, and so, with her being familiar with my clips, she called me. One busy assignment led to three more, and eventually, I became a regular contributing writer. This accomplishment was more than favorable for my career and helped me forward.

A lot of first-time writers get frustrated with the novel and the work that's involved in putting it together. But writing doesn't have to be ruled out for you. Perhaps you just need to do little writing assignments. Writing for various magazines serves as an advantage when you like to write on a variety of topics and in case you come to realize that working on a book isn't for you.

Keep in mind that there are a number of smaller magazines such as *Urban Soul* music magazine geared to African-American music and issues that are always looking for new writers.

It's also good practice to visit the newsstands and bookstores and examine the magazines that are out. You don't always have to write for larger, manuscript-saturated magazines in order to get published.

It's Plain & Simple

It might be difficult to plan paying your mortgage around your freelance magazine assignments, but you will be able to build your career and increase your credibility, creativity, pride and influence. Aim high and after that, aim higher. There are unlimited opportunities once you get your name out there

If you want to get across an idea,
wrap it up in a person.
—Ralph Bunche

Chapter 9
Captivating Your Audience

Being published in a magazine usually implies your extensive knowledge of a subject. Therefore, your proposal package should include three sample chapters, a book outline and of course, your query letter.

You want a magazine editor to notice your work above all others. To do that, you must captivate their attention. The query letter is important as the first step, in order to get your work noticed and understood. It summarizes what your work is about, how many words it has and why it will be of interest to their readers. The query letter is usually short and simple and should get straight to the point.

Be Clear

The letter is almost like a resume or business proposal. You cannot, or shouldn't be long-winded and it shouldn't go beyond one page. Time is of the essence, and you have to be as straightforward as possible.

Basic Tips

When you submit a proposal, it is preferable that you are an expert, such as: a licensed psychiatrist, doctor, teacher, trainer, nurse, social worker, care giver specialist or any trained instructor or specialist.

If you are pitching an excerpt from your book about the spirituality of yoga, you must first focus on the main theme and why the readers are going to be interested. A sample letter might look like this:

Susan Smith
Articles Editor
Go-Get Magazine
2454 Letters Lane
W. New York, NY 00000

Dear Ms. Smith:

Yoga is the latest trend today. No longer an affluently white cultural interest, Yoga has crossed the color barrier. The spiritual essence Yoga provides to African-American women is gaining new access and acceptability.

The enclosed excerpt entitled, "Karma Magic", explores the reasons why we should seek yoga.

Since you are a magazine centered on empowering women, I believe this article will be helpful and benefit your readers.

I look forward to hearing your response to my article of 1,000 words.

Sincerely,

Jane B. Mona

The Proposal

Magazine editors who might consider non-fiction articles and novels for publication commonly request a proposal.

I actually made this mistake when I presented a non-fiction book to a magazine for publishing. It was about relationships, and I was cautioned that it would be difficult to sell because I was not a relationship expert. I had experienced many mishaps with my past relationships and heard of many mishaps from my girlfriends; but, of course, I was not licensed and therefore was not considered an expert on the matter.

Just because someone like your Aunt Susie may have told you, will really not mean a thing to a publisher. So you have to also provide a *brief* bio, no more, than half a page, listing your credentials, as follows.

Authors' Short Bio

Lillian Lola is a licensed physical therapist who focuses on sports injury rehabilitation. She is a co-chairperson on the Natural Rehabilitation Society in Chicago, Illinois, as well as being an advocate for recovery issue.

Ms. Lola travels the world, and works with the National Basketball Association as project coordinator for their rehabilitation program.

She currently resides in New York.

It is essential to include a synopsis with each work/article that you submit and an objective of what the reader is supposed to get out of this. Also, submit your first three sample chapters and a brief synopsis:

Be Thorough

▼ Always, make sure to have your manuscript typed, double-spaced and go over your contents once or twice.

▼ You can customize your submissions to suit the publication. Improvise and include whatever you feel is pertinent to you, but the bottom line is to keep it short.

▼ *The Writer's Market*, which is published by *The Writer's Digest*, contains further examples of how you can pattern your query letters.

The synopsis is a quick overview of the entire project. In one to two pages, you must be able to give a summary of your work. Ask yourself if the following points are included:

▼ Who are the main characters?
▼ What is the central theme of the story/article?
▼ What are the main points entailed?
▼ Do you briefly describe the beginning, middle and the end?
▼ Summarize the main points only.
▼ Leave the ending open, making the editor wanting more.
▼ Stay clear to the point of the story.

Example

> *The Tale* is a journey between two people, a man and a woman, one black and one Hispanic, who find themselves in love and at the crossroads of their careers. When the two fall in love, there is much more to happen as they collide with passion, lust, intrigue and desire.

They live in Los Angeles until the city turns dangerous and becomes filled with turmoil. When 23-year-old Yolanda Lewis relocates to Cincinnati, Ohio in the heat of the riots that follow the death of a nineteen-year old unarmed black man by a racist white cop, Yolanda and Hector Rodriquez (a cop) find themselves on the opposite side of the fence.

The Tale is poignant and gritty, combining the truth about racial politics, life and love.

This type of synopsis should always be included when you're pitching an idea to an editor. In this sample, the readers are expected to pay attention to the budding love story between this young black woman and the Hispanic cop at her side. The theme is intriguing because many may want to know what happens.

Please don't rush. Believe it or not, you have your own deadline. And amongst the myriad of chores and other duties you have to complete, getting a manuscript done may seem like one of the most difficult things in the world. There's never enough time. You must always remember that.

Self Check

In writing my synopsis, I changed it many times before I felt it was suitable for submission.

Because you only have two pages maximum in order to say what you must, it's easy to feel pressured.

Hopefully, your synopsis will be the interesting piece that entices the editor into wanting to publish your work of art. Just to recap:

▼ Take the time to gather your thoughts, as you should.

▼ Don't lose sight that your synopsis is only meant to be used as a guideline, giving the editor an idea of what the total article is about.

▼ Keep it at a page and no more than a page and a half.

Some writers skip the synopsis and only include the details in their cover letter, but usually it is preferable to provide a separate explanation.

Overview

This chapter works for you if you want to send your work out to magazines. But, no matter what you decide to do, it's always good to know your options.

It's Plain & Simple

If you're only going to self-publish your work, it may be helpful for you to just write the synopses and query letter for yourself. This can make it clearer for you to understand your ideas and where you want to go with your book.

*Everybody keeps telling me how surprised they are with
what I've done. But I'm telling you honestly that it
doesn't surprise me. I knew I could do it.*
—Patrick Ewing

Chapter 10
Your First Sale...And Beyond

If you use magazines as a vehicle, they can help you with your self-published efforts...both emotionally and financially.

You've followed the rules and won. Congratulations! A magazine is interested in your book; and they've accepted your writing project. Your books just got delivered from the printer and your uncle came to your home to buy one. Happily, your first sale comes with an indefinable elation.

Your very first sale of your work is important and special in that it is establishing you as a writer. Carrying your first check, no matter what the amount, is one that you earned. What you have accomplished is what many writers sometimes spend a lifetime seeking—publication.

Making It Count
What you want to do with your first check is entirely up to you, of course, but you should try to make it extra special by doing something out of the ordinary or investing in a savings account or even a brokerage account.

The incentive is not entirely financial, but rather a motivating factor for you. This is a sign that you can accomplish all of your goals and it will push you into writing more and going that extra mile.

I thought I would include some tips on actually what to do with that money now that is has started rolling in, or will soon be rolling in. It may seem a little bit off the subject, but this is as important as getting published.

The Nature of Investing

In this country, there are a disproportionate number of white Americans who have investment knowledge that seemingly isn't offered to African-Americans. Although the stock market made many investors leery after the September 11th attacks, most people are finding a renewed belief in the financial market.

Although you should try to see a financial investor for further information on investing basics, it doesn't take a genius to know that many African-Americans need to know more about how to start saving their money and where. The stock market involves a certain amount of risk that many of us have been afraid to dive into.

Self Check

You'll discover that without risk, there is sometimes very little to gain. Try to get used to taking risks, because many of us don't, out of fear.

You can invest in a number of stocks, bonds, mutual funds, or plain old savings and checking accounts (although they don't yield very high interest rates). If you're a little rocky about investing in the beginning, then stash some money away in a piggy bank, or something. But don't blow all the money you've started to make.

This business is very tricky and a certain amount of success does not guarantee a lifetime of success. Open up a bank account with that first amount of money you make on your book. I wouldn't preach it if I weren't practicing it myself. It's time that African-Americans begin to accumulate the wealth that has seemingly been denied us.

Not all of us are athletes or entertainers who make a lot of money each year. And, we don't have to be millionaires in order to get a piece of the big pie that's out here. Don't be intimidated by reports on how bad the economy is doing or how disadvantaged you are because of your race or economic background. There is money to be made in this country and you are entitled to a big percentage of it.

Don't Rest On Your Laurels

It's easy to get a case of the nerves when it comes to beginning your next book or assignment. Sometimes the first book you release may be so successful that you're afraid you won't be able to top yourself. After you've published that first work and made your first sale or a number of sales, it's easy to freeze up.

If you happen to release a worldwide bestseller in the very beginning of your career, that book will be a tough act to follow. Your first bestseller is going to make a name for you in the industry, but it doesn't mean you should slack off when it's time for you to deliver your second book.

Don't get so sidetracked by the influx of money that you forget you have other works to invest your time in. Money, if not handled properly, can go just as easily as it came and then you'll find yourself back at square one, not exactly the best place for you to be.

Share Your Accomplishments

This is something that so many writers neglect to do. Go and volunteer your spare time at a local library by holding a discussion group for other writers. Or, teach a course about writing basics at an adult high school program. It's important for you to remain an inspiration to other writers who have not been published before.

First of all, it's the other struggling writers and avid readers that got you where you are. Don't neglect them or they may neglect you in the future, which will result in lower book sales.

Something To Think About

Many writers tend to forget where they came from after they've 'made' it. All of a sudden, they're looking for talk shows and flossing and glossing at book signings. How quickly these writers forget that they were once on the other end, begging for a book deal. And all of a sudden they've forgotten the integrity that got them to where they are.

Take a few minutes out of your time to be appreciative and thankful because, no matter what God you follow or what religion, if any, there is one principal that seems to hit every nationality and person regardless of his or her race or religion. You do reap what you sow.

Be respectful of those people you saw on the way up because you might just see them on the way down.

Consider Public Speaking, Too

Think about the last booksigning that you attended. Was it a famous author? Perhaps it was E. Lynn Harris? Brenda Thomas? Walter Moseley? Mary Morrison? What drew you into their presentation? Was it the way they told their story? Their overall charisma? Their confidence? Think about their approach, learn from your experience and apply yourself toward gaining the fame and fortune you desire.

Now that you've begun to establish yourself as an author, this might be a good time to begin or expand your writing career to include public speaking career. A well-planned presentation will help you secure your book buying audience and attract new clients. Be considerate of your audience and always keep your presentation on a professional level.

Always plan your message strategically, the content of your book or your writing style. Allow your personality to dictate the delivery of your message; don't try to become someone else. Humor can be good, but not on every occasion. Watch your language—regardless of the topic.

Practice with a tape recorder so you can learn to control the sound and pitch of your voice, and be emphatic about your message.

Here are some tips for planning your presentation.

- ▼ Include a message that your audience will remember and repeat to others.
- ▼ Know who your audience is and give them the information they want.
- ▼ Dressing appropriately for the subject matter and the occasion.
- ▼ Work on your gestures so you don't send an inappropriate signal.
- ▼ Control your voice and speak with passion and sincerity.
- ▼ Don't be afraid to share your personal experiences.
- ▼ If you have characters in your book, bring them to life.

Have a conversation with your audience. Include them in your presentation. Always try to draw them into your message, so you get the results you want...laughter, tears...and of course, a standing ovation.

Start Writing Immediately

You should start writing well before your next deadline approaches. Since this is the craft you desire, pursue it at all costs. Don't wait to write. Do it whenever you get the chance. Write as often as possible. Not only will you meet all your deadlines, but you'll also keep those fingers working and you'll keep on being creative.

Keep those juices flowing so that you'll have less procrastination and writer's block. Once you stumble into complaining about not being able to write anything, the words will be harder to come by.

Celebrate With Your Peeps

The same people you worked so hard to sell your book to—those church folk, all those sisters at the local hair salon—invite them to a celebration party. Since you've sold your book and managed to have an amount of success from it, due to these people, it's time that you showed them appreciation for buying your book.

You can even send out a mass e-mail to those who've given you their web address and thank them that way. It doesn't have to be anything big, a simple gathering at your place or the local bookstore that's willing to let you in their space now that you're a known published author. Try to do something to show these people that you're grateful.

Make Your Fans Feel Special

You can do this by setting up a fan club or a newsletter which lets your fans know of your next book. It makes them feel as if they're in on what you're doing and a part of your success, as well they are.

A number of romance writers use this technique to keep their readers informed as to what is going to be the next published book before anyone else knows. It keeps the readers in touch with you and may even create more of a fan base for you in the long run.

Simply get a list (it could be small) of those who've published your book or have come to your book signing. It will cost them nothing to subscribe and it's another good way of strengthening the respect of your fans.

It's Plain & Simple

The most important thing is to enjoy your first sale and make the most of it. Hopefully, you'll have many more sales to look forward to. And as long as you don't spend your money like someone crazy and neglect your fans, this is only the beginning. This is the special part because it is the motivation to pull you further. Enjoy it!

Set your goals high and don't stop until you get there.
—Bo Jackson

Chapter 11
Working With Agents

Many established writers have initially tried the route of getting their material sent to major book publishers at their own cost and expense. So what's the point? I'll get to that in a minute, but the fact is, most major publishers require you to work with an agent. I want this chapter to dispel and demystify the myth versus the reality of working with agents.

This is a decision that most writers are always up in the air about. Many writers are unaware about agents and even more unsure about using them. Because of this, I chose to pay particular attention to agents.

First and foremost, it's best to pay attention to the following steps if you wish to know how the publishing industry flows on a daily basis.

1. First, you may or may not approach an agent. Most writers usually do and for those of you that are self-publishing, this step isn't in your agenda.

2. You and your agent have a mutual agreement to work together on your book, discussing any ideas about it and sharing the concerns you may have on any updates or adjustments needed.

3. After your agent works with you on any corrections and/or changes and you submit the revised version of your manuscript, it's on to the next step.

4. You agent believes in you, loves your work and decides he/she wants to represent you to the fullest. Now the job begins in getting the book to a publisher.

5. Your agent will send you a contract, which should be looked at carefully before you choose to work with them. A relationship with an agent is much like a marriage and should be thought out carefully before going ahead on it. This person is going to be handling your affairs and dealing with your money so you better be sure before you pursue this relationship further.

6. If you agree to the terms the agent has laid down in front of you, then and only then do you send them back confirmation, with your signature.

7. It is up to your agent to shop the manuscript or your proposal to publishers, giving them a week or two to review it. It's best that your agent believes in you and is a good salesperson as well. Your agent should be able to convince the publisher that your work is hot and stands out from the rest and should be strongly considered. You shouldn't be underestimated and your agent should give you 'mad props' every time he or she speaks about your work.

8. If there are a lot of publishers who are interested, your agent should make sure that your manuscript will go to the highest 'bidder'. Whoever is going to offer you the best deal should get first dibs on your work.

9. Once the publisher agrees to take on your work, a contract is sent to your agent and the two of you go over it. It's best to have a lawyer that you trust in on the deal as well. This just makes it easier during negotiations, to make sure you're getting a deal that is sound.

10. After everything is explained and you consent and agree to the contract, you and your agent are pushed into the next

level. The agent gets the complete contract and you sign it. Once that's done, if there is an advance (where in most deals there is), your agent will receive an advance check and will take out a 10% or 15% commission. Your agent will then forward the balance to you.

11. Receiving an advance is one of the most rewarding parts, but the best is yet to come after your agent sends the finished work to the publisher. They approve it and your agent usually gets the second half of the advance installment. Then on average, a year to up to two years later, the book receives promotion and is published.

12. Here is the best and final part. It is on the bookshelves and you can call up all your friends and family and celebrate your accomplishments. This is the most gratifying of all. As you can see, the publishing process is a long road of twists and turns and it doesn't happen overnight.

Why Is An Agent Necessary?

Politics is the most common reason for getting an agent. But no one will tell you this. The fact of the matter is, writing is big business and the volume of manuscripts that any publisher receives, can be staggering. It is impossible for any publisher to weed through all the manuscripts.

Whether the publisher has two assistants or an entire staff of twenty assistants, they can't possibly get to the thousands of manuscripts they receive and most may require several readings.

So, the agent is really nothing more than a middleman. Most publishers and editors seek out agents who are reputable and can truly say that a writer is talented. Now, the reason for this is that it cuts through the amount of time that they'd have to spend reading all the manuscripts themselves.

Something To Think About

A writer with an agent is seen as being more reputable. And, this is because the publisher has a working relationship with the agent already. Therefore, when publishers say they don't accept unsolicited manuscripts, they actually mean they don't accept those writers who don't have agents.

Agents are meant to be your voice. Some writers do not like dealing with finances or don't want to be bothered with anything other than writing.

An agent is also good for the writer who gets easily intimidated or confused with contracts. So, if you aren't a mathematician and you're wondering how to manage the first big book deal, an agent might be what you're looking for.

That Money Thing

The first rule that one must remember is that nothing in life is free. Hiring an agent also comes with a financial price. Say that you land that six-figure book deal. You're all ready to expect that phat (large) check that's going to allow you to be set for life. But there is one thing you have to remember first.

Your Agent has to get paid too. In this case, it's usually 10-15% of the amount you receive. This includes your advance, which is your initial payment, and all royalties made on subsequent sales of your book. And other expenses that can be included with an agent are the cost of postage, copying, reprints and international fees, which is in case your work is sold or picked up outside the United States.

This is why many writers should and must (unless you want to run the risk of really getting ripped off), review your contracts carefully and consult a lawyer, should you not feel confidant or you suspect the deal you're getting is not feasible. A lawyer can review the terms with you and decide whether or not you're really getting played.

So, Why Get An Agent?

This decision is up to you and in the eye of the beholder. More than a few writers get published without an agent. So, if it works for you or sounds like something that fits into your goals, then you should strongly consider getting an agent.

Self Check

You should get an Agent if:

▼ You do not want to be involved with financial matters.

▼ You don't have time to get involved with financial matters.

▼ You would rather focus solely on writing.

▼ You want to have the agent act as a middleman to properly handle your business.

▼ You have established a professional and personal relationship with the agent and trust that he or she will get a deal that meets your wants and needs.

▼ You want publishers to personally consider your work right away.

Any number of these reasons will do if you're considering an agent.

Getting An Agent, Finally

Many times rejection is not a sign that you're not a good writer, rather that your work doesn't meet the current market standards.

So sometimes having a reputable agent is actually somewhat of a large help. That is, as long as your agent is well known and has a good track record. And that means that your agent has to know all the right people...people who are going to get your work in print.

The problem with this is a really good agent is very hard to find without being personally referred to one. There are plenty of agents out there who will claim to know all the right people, but they don't. And this can lead to no money, as well as long and consuming legal problems. Agents usually receive commissions of 10% or 15% for book publishing deals; and sometimes even higher percentages depending on specific television, foreign and movie rights.

One Writer's Experience
**Tonya Belvin

I heard it was hard to get an agent. So when I started working as an assistant editor at a women's magazine, I went to my editor-in-chief and asked her for suggestions. Luckily she referred three agents to me. I sent all three of them samples and heard a positive response from one of them.

Immediately we started working together. I signed a contract and then he proceeded to tell me how he thought my manuscript was definitely a best seller and that he was going to start sending it out.

Suddenly, when he was going to send my sample chapters out, I discovered that I had to pay for all the postage. I thought it was strange, but when he mailed his letterhead to me, I had to send it out to the designated publishers.

I did this for a while and a year and a half later there had been numerous rejections and no positive responses. In almost two years he wasn't able to sell any of my work. Convinced that something didn't seem right, I decided to terminate my contract.

After doing some research, it occurred to me that not only did he not give me any feedback, but he didn't keep in constant touch with me either. Sometimes I wouldn't hear from him for months.

He quickly agreed when I terminated our agreement in writing.

After that, I called one of the other agents on my list. She agreed to take another, closer look at my book. Soon she gave me substantial feedback, told me of the corrections I needed to make and explained she wouldn't send me a contract unless she was a hundred percent sure she could sell my work to a major publisher.

I felt like such a fool because I wasted two years and there was no response. I spent so long with an agent who really didn't know many industry folks and was making me do all the work.

I was so eager to get my work published that I put up with this slack guy because I kept hoping he would eventually sell my stuff. I mean, I thought since he stood to profit off of me, that he was going to work hard for me.

Now I have a new agent, but I have lots of work to do to my manuscript in order to make it sellable. And since I wrote this novel over three years ago, it needs a number of revisions. I'm a little ashamed of the two years wasted, but I'm praying I get things right this time.

Agent Knowledge

What Tonya went through is common. But there are other horror stories, writers who've even paid fees to agents. Never. Never send any money to an agent to be considered. If you have to pay them, more than likely they are not to be trusted.

You don't have to pay anyone in order to get your work read. Also, when it's time for you to read and examine contracts, make sure you have a lawyer present. Certain contracts are written in such confusing terms, that you don't understand what is technically going on. Therefore, a disreputable agent can make a contract out so that they make most of the money and you are left with the remainder—little to nothing.

Basic Tips
One good guide to check out agents is *Literary Agents: A Writer's Guide* by Adam Begley. (Published in association with Poets & Writer's Inc.) It clues you in on all the basics. Another guide is the *Writer's Market*, which contains some information on agents as well.

An agent is supposed to help you make the publishing process go smoothly and well. If you're having problems communicating or working together at any point in time, look at the clause in your contract and see what it says about you terminating your relationship.

Anyone you're going to trust with your money should have your best interest at heart; and, it's not hard to tell when they don't. Use your instincts; but it is best to read up on them first and make sure they are reputable. Look and see what authors they have worked with and who they've gotten published. Are those authors anyone you've ever heard of? Do you like the books of the authors that got published?

Common sense will have to guide you through this whole process. Remember to carefully screen an agent after you've decided on one. There are ways to investigate an agent to make sure they're reputable and going to do the work they promised to do for you

Remember, the business of writing is all about making money and if you can't deliver, then the future of your writing career with the publishing house is in question. If you're book does well or just mediocre, then you may find yourself getting another book deal. However, if your book flops and doesn't do well at all, your writing career well may be over with them, as well as with your agent. They won't give you another chance to get published if your work doesn't sell. You can never forget that bottom line when you go with a mainstream publisher. It's all about the dollar bill and if your work doesn't produce that, they can't continue to work with you in the long run.

Even if you swear that your next series of works will be much better. The risk may be too great to give you that second chance after they've lost so much money.

Maybe you are not familiar with legal terminology or have never consulted a lawyer in your neighborhood. However, if you are considering making any major financial moves, then you should really consult someone professional.

Consult A Lawyer, If You Need To

When getting your advances and royalty checks, with or without an agent, you have to keep track of your money. Many writers feel they have been used and underpaid because they were not informed about the details of their publishing contracts and any fees that would be deducted from their payments.

Things like this will leave you broke. So, going for a local legal consultation isn't half bad an idea. Most attorneys are willing to work with you for a small fee and will usually assist you for as long as you require it.

Getting An Agent After Self-Publishing

Most writers pray to deliver a work like *The Invisible Man* as their first book. However, most are not faced with such success as the late Ralph Ellison was.

Some works gain popularity slowly. Such is the case of Teri Woods' successful book *True To The Game*. Her work has gained attention nationwide and made Essence magazine's best seller list, as well. But she's one of the many writers who self-published initially; it's even rumored that she sold her books out of the trunk of her car.

Sometimes your book can become so vastly popular that it eventually catches the attention of a mainstream publisher. Once that happens, you have the option of getting an agent or not. But, not all best-selling authors have agents. And, just because you're a best-selling author now, doesn't mean that the company doesn't want you to have an agent. Some publishers feel more comfortable working with an agent.

But if an agent isn't your thing, you can use the assistance of a lawyer, although most lawyers don't usually act as a liaison between a writer and his/her publisher.

Not having an agent is **almost** unheard of in mainstream publishing. The deal with agents is pretty simple and straightforward. Weigh the pros and cons and then make your decisions from there.

Self Check

The following questions can help you iron out any concerns you might have. Make sure when you answer them, that they all suit you.

1. The agent should discuss his or her expectations with you. What do they expect you to bring to the table?

2. Some contracts are verbal. If you don't agree with this, ask if you could get a written contract. Ask for a copy of the contract to keep for yourself.

3. Ask the agent if they consult with you and their other clients on all offers, or just on some. It's also good to ask if they let you know of all rejections and acceptance letters. Remember, if you like to be kept informed, then you really want to know these things upfront. Some writers complain about not being informed on things they think they should know.

4. Another question you should ask is what is their editorial input? That is, do they look at your manuscript and make any corrections, objections, or grammar/spelling corrections. Some agents only make spelling corrections and not advisements on story content. If you want an agent's honest opinion on your work, ask them!

5. You need to know how your agent operates. Do they have assistants, or partners, or do they work alone? If they work alone, you'll have to understand that it may take longer for them to get your work out.

6. Ask what the commissions are for other than U.S. sales, such as movie and television rights as well as foreign rights of your work. As a matter of fact, you should know this from the very beginning. The amount of money they get affects the amount of money you get.

7. Ask how soon after getting your book deal are payments dispersed to you.

8. Agents also charge clients for certain expenses like postage and photocopying. Ask if they do this.

9. Most important on your mind should be how long they have been an agent, if they are willing to provide you with a listing of their other clients, and if they are a member of the Association of Authors' Representatives. It will put your mind at ease to know how reliable they are.

10. Know who handles your work at all times, if you're with a large agency. Make sure you know who your agent's assistant is and what they do for him/her.

11. Ask them if they issue you yearly 1099 tax forms. It's important to keep your paperwork straight and organized so you can avoid any tax problems.

12. Another important but difficult thing to do is to plan out what to do with your cash in the event of your death. Probably including a financial advisor, in this case, is the wisest thing to do. Who is going to handle your royalties and what will happen should you die before another book gets published?

    Most writers make the mistake of not asking the most vital questions and can find matters getting messy when things change for the worst. Since life is about change, you should always try to stay two steps ahead in this game.

13. Last, but not least, ask about how you will receive money if the two of you part ways. Some agents require you to give thirty days notice. Others make sure that they still receive any monies associated with a book they sold just prior to your departure. It's important to ask as relationships constantly change and you could find your work agreement change at any time. Some agents may be pleasant to work with in the beginning and suddenly may change over time.

Be Aware

Hate to have to get to this point, but it is a possibility, so it must be covered. As with the good in anything, comes the bad. Since there are so many writers striving to get published, there are also tons of agents pushing themselves off to eager literary geniuses, such as yourself.

Therefore, many agents are actually con artists. They ask you for a fee and then run off with your money. No reputable agent should ask you for a dime. They will make plenty of money off of you, once a publishing house takes your book. After all, their main purpose is to get you a book deal.

So, there are many so-called agents who will not deliver, or if they do, it will only be to their advantage. I had once worked with an agent that simply held my manuscripts for months, and that turned into a year, and longer. Eventually, I had to write him a formal letter, stating that I wished to terminate my contract and self-publish my book.

I, on the other hand, got out of that contract, after giving thirty days notice, and I ended up taking my novel to another agent who has faithfully agreed to represent it; and I'm still hoping my novel will be in bookstores soon, as the result of our working relationship.

It's Plain & Simple

Getting an agent is always an option. It's up to you if that's the way you choose to go. Because , when an agent is very good, they're a good asset to have. They can save time and help you if you don't want to be bothered with the business matters.

We've removed the ceiling above our dreams.
There are no more impossible dreams.
—Jesse Jackson

Chapter 12
Understanding the Contract

Understanding the publishing contract may seem like the most difficult thing. If you're self-publishing your first book under you own imprint, then you can tailor the contract the way you see fit. But if you're working under any other means to put your book out, there is always a contract accompanying it; and it's best you understand the ins and outs of things now, beforehand.

Most people would recommend that you hire an attorney before signing and agreeing to the contract. There may be a number of things you don't agree with, but if you sign it, that contract is legally binding. So, you can't go back later talking about how you want to change your mind. We'll explore just some of the basic terminology to get you acquainted with what a contract might be really saying.

You may not be in this industry solely for the money, but now that you are making it, you should manage it properly so that you can keep as much as possible.

First, we're going to look at a contract you might sign with an agent, if you choose to get one. It's pretty basic and is only an example of what an agent can offer you.

An Agent's Contract
An agent's contract is going to say some pretty basic things. But all of the following may or may not be addressed. Such amendments to

this agreement are up to the individual writer. When going through your contract, you can read and compare whether or not your own contract contains such information.

▼ The agent agrees, to the best of his or her ability, to market and submit your work to publishers that they feel are best qualified to represent you. The agent assumes no responsibility for the response of the publisher, and will notify you if a publisher rejects the proposal for your book.

▼ The agent agrees to pay for all shipping, copying and office costs in the promotion of said writer(s)' work. All fees shall be reimbursed to the agent at such time a contract is signed by the writer with a publisher.

▼ The agent agrees to represent the writer in all work(s) the writer provides within a three- (3) year period.

▼ Once said work(s) are accepted by a publisher, the agent agrees to receive 15% of royalties, thereafter, distributing the remaining to the writer. Usually, a 20% commission is charged for all TV, movie and foreign rights.

▼ The agent agrees to work for the best possible financial deal, on behalf of the writer, and inform the writer of any and all agreements that are agreed to.

▼ The agent reserves the right to reject certain publishing deals, which they feel do not represent the best interest of the writer. (For instance, if an agent feels he or she can get more money for your work, then they reserve the right to reject the wrong publishing deal.)

▼ Either the agent or the writer may terminate this agreement, at any given time, with a written thirty- (30) day notice. The agent is entitled to receive any monies for deals, which are current, or any deals for the writer who they were responsible for setting up before the writer submitted notice.

Be Thorough

Many writers and other creative professionals have gotten themselves into financial contracts where they have found themselves on the wrong end of the stick. And for all your hard work, the least you deserve is to get the most from your work. It hurts more to realize that you did all the work and your agent got all the residuals.

There are a number of other clauses and terms that may or may not be included in the deal between the writer and the agent. These are just a few of the points a typical contract may include. Understanding a contract is all a matter of simply reading, and trying to grasp the language of it all.

Perhaps what might help you is describing what you should expect to see in a contract. The following contains the most basic information that you should look for whenever you sign any contract, whether it is for a publisher or an agent.

The list is as follows:

Dates: The date the agreement is entered upon usually appears somewhere at the beginning or the end of the contract. It just states that on a certain date, you and the publisher formally made the publishing agreement. Your address should also be listed.

Parties: This identifies the name and addresses of the publisher, and the name and address of the author. It clearly states who the publisher is, as well as whom the author is.

Title: The said or tentative title of the manuscript is then listed here. The title may be tentative in the event the author has made an agreement, but has not agreed on the title of the book as of yet.

License to Publish: This states that the author has agreed to give the publisher the right to publish their work in print and the parties have agreed to all the contents of the publishing contract.

Grants of Rights: This can vary. Some publishers may agree only to publish your work in English while others agree to publish in a number of languages. It may also allow the publisher to publish, sell and distribute the work in all forms including audio on CD, and on the Internet. In short, the author retains all the publication rights not granted to the publisher.

Delivery of the Manuscript: Herein describes any specific date a manuscript is promised to a publisher and the length of the manuscript, as well as any additional contained information, such as illustrations, etc. Usually a writer will have a deadline by which they must deliver the manuscript in its entirety.

Term: For a number of publishers, they have a certain amount of time by which they promise to publish your book. It may be anywhere from two to three years, or more. The time specified is entirely up to the publisher.

Additional Materials: The writer may wish to provide further materials in addition to the manuscript: such as photos, additional illustrations or a rough draft for the book's cover. Usually larger publishers have in-house, freelance or contributing illustrators that work for them. A smaller publisher will allow the author to submit an idea of what they want the cover to look like; or the author might know of an illustrator they personally wish to use and submit a rough draft from that illustrator.

Author Cancellation: This clause allows the author to terminate his or her publishing agreement within thirty (30) days to a year. However, many larger publishing houses can legally bind you to a contract, such as the case, with a three-book deal. After you deliver your third book to the publisher, you are then free to leave the agreement, given thirty (30) days notice. This of course, varies on your deal. But this is very, very important.

Oftentimes, you may start out with a particular agreement, but then later, you might change or feel that the publisher has changed, and you might feel that it's time for you to leave the deal. Always look at what it takes to get out of a contract, every time you sign one. It can't be stressed enough.

Something To Think About

So before you sign you name on the dotted line of anything, make sure you understand everything, and I mean everything you've read and most important, even if it's your uncle's lawyer and you trust him to death. But consult someone who will be able to give you some type of advice that could keep you from going broke.

Look for These Clauses in Every Contract You Sign:

▼ Publish and Submission Acceptance:

Here describes the publisher's agreement to publish the writer's work within a certain period of time. Failure of a publisher to deliver said manuscript at such time could allow the writer to terminate his or her agreement. However, the publishing house may also describe here, its right to terminate your manuscript based upon its own discretion.

▼ **Royalty Payments:**

Herein the publisher describes the amount of royalty payments they may make. Some publishers agree to make four (4) annual payments during a certain calendar period; and, others may break it down to be a little more specific. That is, the publisher may promise a certain percentage on the number of books sold, such as 15% of 5,000 books and so on and so forth. This helps you to know when to prepare to receive your money. It is also important that any agreement you sign is specific about this factor.

▼ **Subsidiary Rights:**

This usually states that the publisher will own all subsidiary and licensing rights. That includes advertising, commercial uses, plays, television, radio and film, as well as reprints and audio, among other formats specified.

▼ **Publication Format:**

This clause indicates whether you or the publisher will be responsible for the appearance, format and production of the book. This, of course, depends on the individual agreement you sign.

▼ **Copyright/Title Registration:**

This certifies that either the publisher or the author separately or jointly owns the rights to the manuscript as well as the title of the manuscript.

▼ **Account Information:**

This states that the publisher will notify you as to the status of your sales, the number of copies of your book that has been sold and the number of copies of your book that has been printed and bound. Usually smaller publishers do this. If you have an agent, this information may be given to them and then the agent will give it to you. Also, the publisher may provide you with the number of books that may have been returned.

▼ **Author Proof:**

The author also has the right to inquire about the nature or status of their royalties and the number of books sold, etc. This is a good clause to look for in the contracts you sign. Not all publishers are created equal and you want to be able to inspect the dealings of your publisher when necessary. In a perfect world, you might not have to worry about information being fraudulent, but in this world, you have to keep on top of your records at all times.

▼ **Author Warranty:**

This states that you warrant that you are the sole creator of the work, which is being published, that it is your original work, and that you own all the rights granted under your agreement. It also certifies that your work doesn't infringe upon anyone else's work, and that you are not currently in another agreement with the same manuscript. You also certify that, as the author, all the information you've submitted is not inflammatory or obscene and does not infringe on any other copyrights.

▼ **Indemnification:**

In the event that the above warranty is breached (that is, not fulfilled and you have actually infringed upon other copyrights, etc.), you therefore may agree to hold the publishers blameless or any of its affiliates from settlements, damages and lost profits, etc. This should be included in every contract you sign. And more likely than not, you're going to see it because it protects the publisher. They have to include this protection because, as with anything, not all writers are created equal and there are some writers out there who purposely try to get 'over'. They may sign a contract with a publisher knowing that they are currently involved in a deal already. Therefore, the publisher is not responsible if any of the information you've provided is incorrect or illegal.

▼ **Notices:**

As previously mentioned, this clause defines the means and the amount of days the author and publisher have to terminate their agreement. This is, and should be included in all contracts because what may fit in your world now might not fit a year from now, and you may need to get out of the contract that currently suits you. Pay close attention to this clause.

▼ **Promotion:**

Sometimes the publishing company likes to use your name and work in its promotions. They may even use your picture and therefore may request that you agree to it. This advertising is well advised because it can help with the sales of your work. Usually writers do not reject this clause.

Although most publishers agree to do the majority of the promotion and advertising, some small and self-publishers may require you to be responsible for advertising your book on your own. That is, you have to schedule your own book signings, readings, Internet ads and press releases.

It's Plain & Simple

Even when you sign a contract with an agent, there are things you have to be aware of. If you have at least a little knowledge, it will help you from getting swindled in the long run. Remember, all contracts are not created equal and if you have any doubt, you should go to a lawyer and seek further help.

My mother taught me very early to believe I could achieve any accomplishment I wanted to.
—Wilma Rudolph

Chapter 13
Getting Your Self-Published Book to the Market

The Market Reference Guide

Now you know how the publishing process works. So, whether you get picked up by a major publishing house or self-publish your own book, marketing is key to your success. In this chapter we'll deal with how to go about marketing, promoting and advertising that self-published book that you worked so hard on.

Public Appearances

Should your work and your name take off and you make a huge following for yourself, then you'll have to manage your public appearances at bookstores, libraries, schools and colleges.

Book signings allow you the opportunity to meet the public. In your appearance, you'll need to be personable and enthusiastic about your work. This is going to project to your fans.

Anything is possible. You must have the faith to believe in your career, knowing that it could take off and you could be ready to take the world on by storm. That's why handling your public appearances with confidence will help push you even further.

The Press Kit

It is best to have this to send to magazines at the beginning of your book release. If you are working with an agent and large publishing house, then your agent can work with you on this.

The press kit is comprised of your photo, bio, a review of your book and a copy of your book if requested, to magazines for review. Most publishing houses will submit a review copy to mainstream and small magazines well before the book is published. This way you can make a magazine's deadline and get put into print by the time your book is released.

The press kit is even good for the new author who may not have achieved phenomenal success. It is good to market yourself even you don't get caught up with a big publisher that is going to handle all the costs.

Stay the Course

Your career is very important to you. You've worked hard for it and earned the success that you are now experiencing. So now that you've come this far, manage it well and don't neglect what you've worked so hard to achieve.

Writer's Guides

A great source for helpful information is the *Writer's Market Online* for those of you who are always surfing the web or e-mailing folks all day. With this guide you will be able to:

▼ Research a guide to literary agents.

▼ Learn who represents specific writers so you can judge if that same agent is suited for your work.

▼ Get updates on new markets.

If browsing the Internet for this information isn't your thing, you can buy the *Writer's Market* book.

Always keep track of where you've submitted your work, as well as the responses you receive.

Another good guide for the poets out there is the *Poet's Market*, edited by Nancy Breen, from *Writer's Digest Books*. Published every year, it is a thorough listing that provides information regarding most recently published poets, the full description of each publication, submission details, the kinds of poetry accepted, as well as samples of poetry that has been accepted.

Basic Tips

▼ Writer's Market Online is a valuable guide for freelance writers; it contains a wealth of information and can be accessed additionally at www.WritersMarket.com

▼ The *Poet's Market* is available at all local bookstores, directly from Writer's Digest Books at 1-800-221-5831 or on-line at writersdigest.com.

Marketing

This is the most important process after your book is published. Most self-publishing businesses have a certain way they're going to advertise your book once you've paid the fee. Some offer you a number of free copies and unlimited availability through the web. Others make your book available through the Internet only, not bookstores.

But, even if your self-publisher gives you the utmost in advertising, you can and should always help to advertise your own work, as well. Be sure to utilize as many mediums as possible. With a good advertising plan, you can find yourself selling more books than you could ever imagine.

Word of Mouth

Perhaps the oldest, simplest and best form of advertising, initially, is word of mouth. Go tell as many folks as you can; tell your parents, friends, co-workers, pastor, and your church congregation. Usually after you tell them, they'll go and tell others and so on and so forth. Word of mouth has brought many books from the underground to the mainstream.

Print It Up

It's quite easy to print up flyers advertising your book. Since there are so many variations, you can use your imagination. But here are some tips:

▼ Make the paper bright. Change form the traditional white paper.

▼ Use bold lettering.

▼ Make your book sound like the coolest thing out there. It's best to use adjectives like 'stunning', 'sexy', or 'controversial'. This of course, depends upon the nature of your work. But you want to keep things upbeat and intriguing. If you need help, an advertising student at a community college may do. Most likely, they'd be glad to test their skills with you, maybe even for very little or no money.

▼ Put your flyers everywhere you can possibly imagine; in local bookstores, hand them out at flea markets, in the supermarket or to people you might strike up a conversation with. Always carry your flyers with you to as many places as possible. If you're in school, pass them out to your classmates. You never know when you might need them.

Don't forget to include prices and where they can be purchased. And keep track of any orders people give you. Make sure you have enough books readily available to distribute to them.

Use the Internet

The Internet is a good means of getting your word out to a vast majority of people. On sites like blackplanet.com, you can develop your own web page devoted to advertising your book. You can also advertise with some of the other online resources listed in the Appendix. For many of these sites, it's free to set up a web page.

There are a number of on-line forums and support groups for African-American writers that will open a means of advertising for you through discussion chat rooms. These sites are also a great inspiration where you can meet and network with other published writers.

Be Thorough

When you log onto AOL, Excite or another search engine, you should enter keyword, 'self-publishing' or 'African-American writers' into your search engine. This should bring up tons of places for you to advertise. Check each website to find out the criteria for sharing your book.

Go To Local Bookstores

Local African-American bookstores are places, which can give you maximum exposure. Not only are they already stocked with other African-American writer's books, but they eagerly welcome works from new African American authors.

The African American bookstores in your community are a good place to start, but you should also check out Essence magazine's listing of African-American bookstores. Essence also provides a listing of the best-selling African-American novels. Hopefully, you'll see your book listed there in the near future.

If you develop a rapport with the storeowners, they will probably invite you to hold a book reading and book signing there. It's a prelude to the phenomenal success you might experience in the future.

It also helps African-American bookstores draw in audiences, and thus, more business.

Start A Book Club

If there are no local black bookstores in your neighborhood willing to sponsor you, then you can hold a book signing yourself, either in your apartment or at a local hall. You can invite all of your friends and co-workers, as well as any other enthusiasts.

Book clubs are vastly popular among African-Americans; and nothing makes a group of avid book club members more excited than having the founder of the bookclub, hosting with his or her own book.

Send Press Kits To Radio Stations

Although radio stations primarily play music, they shouldn't be ruled out as places to promote your book. Some local stations, mainly underground, are good for giving books a quick plug and many radio talk show hosts will interview authors.

Even if you don't get any airtime, it's best to send your book anyway because you never now who may be interested in it at the stations. And going back to that word of mouth thing, the word about your book can circulate throughout the station and get you attention that way. No medium should be ruled out.

Send a Press Kit and Sample Copy To Magazines

An excellent place to advertise and market your book is magazines.

Try not to send it to the Editor-In-Chief, however. Usually Editors-In-Chief are extremely busy. Some don't open their mail but will have their assistants do it. You want to send it to whoever is assigned to put it in the magazines.

Research who the book editor is; but if they don't specifically have a book editor then sending it to the Managing Editor or Assistant

Editor may be just as satisfactory. It's good to send them a copy of your book along with your press kit.

With smaller magazines, one or two people may be running the publication and it might be apropriate to send it to either person. Sometimes, you stand a better chance of getting your book featured in smaller magazines because they might be more community oriented. Avid readers go through books like crazy, and your book may just be the new thing they're looking for.

Open a Table at a Flea Market

Rap artist Master P once sold his albums out of the trunk of his car. It was a means that inspired others who followed him to do the same.

Set up shop. If there's a local market, you can do it by setting up your own stand. Flea markets and festivals come to almost every city and town. If you have toiled over your book from scratch, then you can also sell it yourself.

Rent a Booth at an Expo

Book Expo America is the largest national book expo in America for Booksellers (Wholesalers, Distributors, Bookstores). Now, there's an African-American Publishers Pavilion (see Appendix) at the BEA specifically for African-American publishers to feature and display their book(s).

Two other great expos to exhibit at are the American Library Association and the Black Caucus American Library Association which brings in an audience of thousands of Acquisitions / Collections Librarians from all over the United States. And, don't forget the Harlem Book Fair in New York City and now taking place, as well, in Cleveland as a part of the George Fraser's Powernetworking Conference. For those of you on the East Coast, the International Black Buyers & Manufacturers Expo & Conference (IBBMEC) out of Washington, DC is another great starting point for your new publishing business.

You should sign up to display your book(s) at as many local African-American sponsored expos and street fairs as your budget and time will allow. The national expos will require more time and more money, but you may even be able to cut down on the costs b sharing a booth with another author or book publisher.

Consider Mail Order
You can set this up by printing up your own catalog and making your book available by special order. This way you're in control of who gets your book and how soon. It's also easier to keep tabs on your sales.

Set up a P.O. Box at the post office, so you can get orders there rather than having them come directly to your home address. It's good for a start-up business.

Maintain a Database of All Your Contacts
Get a Business Card from everyone you meet…everywhere and put them in a database for your mailing list. Always hand your contact information back to the people you meet and make sure it mentions your book…a business card, a postcard, a bookmark, a flyer, a brochure or a newspaper clipping. To help you begin your mailing list, I've included a listing of resources in Appendix B.

It's Plain & Simple
Getting the word out to the masses can make all the difference between winning and losing. So, now that you know, put in the effort, and you'll never look back.

Your goals are the road maps that guide you and show you what is possible for your life.
—Les Brown

Epilogue

I wrote this book because I think that it is important writers, especially beginning African-American writers, not be intimidated by this hectic and demanding career. I hope it has helped you gain more insight as a new writer.

Perhaps you're not so new to the writing industry and just wanted to cover your bases to make sure you're confident with what you already know.

I began my career as a creative writing major in the ninth grade at Rosa Parks Fine Arts High School. When I started my poetry and working on by-lines and sub-titles for the yearbook, I was constantly criticized by one of my journalism teachers. For years, I just knew I didn't have what it took to make it.

Then I wrote freelance throughout college; and three years after graduation, I began furthering my career. I had met a number of *Vibe* writers and editors at a benefit dinner one evening. Everyone knew everyone else. I was the simple one, not putting on any airs, but just beginning to write. Needless to say, I was snubbed and dissed at that dinner, but I was determined to not be discouraged because I didn't fit into the writers' click.

As I sat at the large table with them, I wondered how many other writers were also intimidated by the fact that they were outside of the secret society. Writing can sometimes be like a private click. When you want to write and get published so badly but it never happens, it's too easy to get discouraged.

Quite often, if the rejection doesn't get to you, the poverty does. While I wrote this book, I also did many freelance articles, for which the publication simply did not have the money to pay me. Those were especially tough times. And, I had to make due quite often with many nine to five jobs and squeeze in my freelance writing when I could.

But, I've always loved to write and it has been my heart's desire every since I could remember. So, throughout this rocky ride to deliver words, new meaning, and thought to the community, you sometimes have to suffer a little. But anything worth having is worth working for.

There are many subsequent struggles in being a writer. Time, little or no pay and strict deadlines make it seem, whether or not, worthless at times—but it isn't. The key to sticking with this writing game is to do it for the sake of communicating, getting your point across.

Now, you may often hear "Black people don't read anymore." But we are reading and it is important that we keep writing in order to keep each other informed and enlightened.

The success of Terry McMillan's book, *Waiting to Exhale*, came immediately after many publishers (mostly white) believed that African-Americans didn't really read, so there was no need to market books to us.

However, when the book became outrageously popular, publishers scrounged to rake up the dollars which spurned a lot of 'copy-cat' writers who all ran to work on similar tales of 3 to 4 women and their difficulties with friendships and black men. All of a sudden we were marketable and everyone was ready to cash in.

And, although the biz seems open, do not be fooled! There is still a much longer road for us to travel. For every one man or woman who may get their books published, there are at least 10 to 15 who don't; endlessly searching for someone to read their work the way a rap artist searches for someone to listen to their demo. It is still difficult.

And you can still walk into a Barnes & Noble and find plenty of white-authored mainstream books, compared to a sometimes significantly small African-American section.

Just recently my publisher Tony Rose/Amber Books finalized an unprecedented pact as the first African-American book publisher to sell its titles directly to the Barnes & Noble Bookstore chain.

So, there is hope that if we keep writing, things will change and the shoe will end up on the other foot. Perhaps I am a bit optimistic, maybe too much so, but it is very, very important that our words are out there.

So as you push on, please refer to as many reference guides as you can. This book is just a small introduction to some of the major players and smaller figures in publishing.

And for those of you who chose to do it yourselves, much love and respect. Your journey will truly be a labor of love as you strive to get those things accomplished that have long since felt like a far away dream. What you want can be a reality if you only allow it to be. Success is waiting for you around the corner. So greet it, meet it.

Naturally the life of a writer isn't glamorous; and sometimes eyebrows will raise curiously when you tell folks what you do, but never back down from the challenge.

I'm still hoping and praying over my own work in that it may just come to be acknowledged. But those who consider this to be stylish may be a bit fooled. What is required is discipline and lots of time alone. You might have to skip that party because an idea came to you and you have to tap into it now.

That is going to require you to be isolated, pondering over words for hours at a time. Other times, you'll have verbal diarrhea and will have to let the words flow from out of nowhere.

So get writing, and take this as just the first step in truly getting ahead. The writer's guidelines for each of the entailed publications may change at any time so you should always write in advance to find out what is required.

We, as African-American writers must have a voice and must have our say. There are many opportunities for screenwriters, playwrights, songwriters, and beyond. But, we have to make sure we start small, aim high, and continue. The pen may not be mightier than the sword, but it is just as sharp. Happy Writing!

—Takesha Powell

Appendix A
Websites: Resources for Authors & Self-Publishers

African-American Companies and Services

AALBC.COM

The African-American Literature Book Club's goal is to increase everyone's knowledge of the diversity of African American literature, facilitate the exchange of opinions, satisfy your on-line book buying needs and serve as a resource and vehicle of expression for aspiring and professional writers.

You may learn about authors, read book excerpts and listen to poetry. You may also learn about popular new books and classic titles. Visit our on-line discussion boards, enter contests and read about up coming events—plus so much more! AALBC.com is a recognized source of critical reviews of books by and about African American Authors.

Aamystery.com

The African-American mystery page contains information of new releases, authors and a reference list of suspense, crime and mystery fiction from African Americans.

Also, great links to other mystery sites, more book sites, and other Internet interests.

Afronetbooks.com

Contains a monthly column for aspiring artists with good information. Book reviews are available and other popular culture interests of African-Americans.

Great for info on everything from black cook books, business books, black bookstores, book clubs, and black publishers. But a most helpful is a link to self-published works, coming very soon to the site. You can also advertise your publishing company here if you're interested.

ALA.org

The American Library Association is the oldest and largest library association in the world, with more than 64,000 members. Its mission is to promote the highest quality library and information services and public access to information. They hold annual events that offer small press (book publishers) a table to showcase their book(s) to thousands of librarians from all over the world.

Amazon.com

Amazon.com is one of the best sites to check out what's new on the market. You can purchase a variety of books, including out of print books. This is very useful for keeping up with the market and on certain books, so that you'll know if you're on the right track. Check out covers, colors and content. Getting your book on Amazon.com should be a priority.

Amberbooks.com

Amber Communications Group, Inc.s' imprint AMBER BOOKS is the nation's largest African-American self-help and career guide publishing house and the recipient of the Chicago Black Book Fair and Conference Independent Publisher/Press Award of the Year and the 2003 ALA Reluctant Reader Award and the 2003 BlackBoard Bestseller's African-American Publisher of the Year Award.

The Company's goal is to build a strong catalog pertaining to and about the African-American experience. They continue to expand with its celebrity bio imprint BUSTA BOOKS, its COLOSSUS BOOKS imprint for international personalities and topics, its AMBROSIA BOOKS imprint for great literature, fiction and non-fiction, and AMBER/WILEY BOOKS, a co-publishing/imprint deal with John Wiley & Sons, Inc. for personal finance and beauty books.

BAIP.org

Black Americans in Publishing, Inc. is a non-profit organization which supports the advancement of black professionals and aspirants in all areas of the publishing industry, through career networking, mentorship, and education outreach. These goals are realized through regular meetings, special programs, and publications dedicated to support, enable, and encourage our membership.

BCALA.org

The Black Caucus of the American Library Association serves as an advocate for the development, promotion, and improvement of library services and resources to the nation's African American community; and provides leadership for the recruitment and professional development of African American librarians. They hold bi-annual events that offer small press (book publishers) a table to showcase their book(s) to thousands of librarians from all over the country.

Blackexpressions.com

Here you can get three books for one dollar and save up to fifty percent on book releases. You will also receive a letter from the editor, and other features such as the message board, member reviews, excerpts, author profiles, bestsellers and a shopping basket for your convenience. Everything is handled on-line and you can get a free magazine with book reviews and other special features. This is a really good site to see all of the popular black books on the market.

Blackplanet.com

One of the greatest sites on the net. Great spot to set up message boards, your own free web page, free membership, e-mail address and note board. Helpful articles on current events and various links.

Blackwordsonline.com

In association with Amazon.com, this is a comprehensive site for Black writers along with links on how to get your work published through small publishers, happening columns and reading fiction and discussion groups.

Very exciting, here. You can read chapters from new or established writers. You can also subscribe to this site and get info on events and monthly updates. But the plus is being considered for publishing here. They accept your mini and full-length stories, poems, book reviews and feature articles of black literature and culture. See the site for additional guidelines.

Blackwriters.org

The Black Writers Alliance is known as "the first literary arts magazine online to 'empower, support, educate and inform aspiring and published black writers'".

Black writers can share words through message boards, chat rooms, writing and critique groups, events and discussion lists. Get a free e-mail address and keep informed of events, tips, contests and more. Membership is $25 per year; not bad to receive all this site has to offer including career opportunities, and fellowships and grants as well.

Bn.com

I thought to include Barnes & Noble because it's a good site to check out what's new on the market. You can also browse the site to purchase a variety of books, including out of print books. This is very useful for keeping up with the market and on certain books, you're allowed to read excerpts and chapters. Getting your book on Bn.com should be one of your first goals.

BookExpoAmerica.com

If you are involved in the book publishing industry, BookExpo America is the only industry event where you can experience the entire scope of book publishing from the U.S. and the world—all in one place, all at one time. And, now, you can be a part of the **African-American Pavilion**. Established for African-American Publishers by African-American Publishers, The African-American Pavilion is the showcase of books and magazines by black publishers or black interest titles, including fiction, non-fiction, children's, self-help and magazines. This is the first ever showcase where the largest exhibit of independently owned African-American publishers is present at Book Expo. Numerous promotions and author signings take place daily.

Bookmarket.com

Provides tips about publishing as well as information on how to market your books. Contains tip of the week and marketing updates, as well as other information of interest. You can order on everything from author's bios to helpful publishing advice.

Bookspot.com

Full of literary criticism, poetry, book reviews, etc. Also a listing of on-line books, and various book facts. You can receive a free newsletter by providing your e-mail address. Great, large list of various links.

Booktalk.com

Contains info on authors, agents, publishers, and bookstores to name a few. Helpful articles on the romance writers industry, reasons for manuscript rejection and query letters as well. This site also provides literary agency references.

Cushcity.com

I included this because of the section they have regarding Self-published author releases. You can sell your book through this site after contacting them at <custsvc@cushcity.com or by mail, phone or fax.

IBBMEC.com

The International Black Buyers and Manufacturers Expo and Conference was created to provide Black retailers, manufacturers, importers, exporters, artists, craftspeople, clothiers and booksellers from throughout the African Diaspora an opportunity to gather once a year for technical training, general business education, trade and networking opportunities. The annual IBBMEC conference is a great place to launch your new book to African-American store-owners, as well as retail customers.

Ipgbook.com

Independent Publishers Group is a book distributor of small and large presses throughout the United States and all over the world.

Find out how to order books, listings by authors, title and publisher as well as the history of IPG. Really insightful of the business of publishing.

Literarymarketplace.com

Check here as a good resource for the book publishing industry. It includes a listing of U.S. International and Small presses and publishers. Also contains a valuable listing of literary agents.

You can also search certain publishers by name, as well as advertising and marketing services, photographers, etc.

Mosaicbooks.com

Launched in 1998, with a desire to showcase and honestly critique African American and Hispanic literature, Mosaic has established itself as an important voice on the literary landscape. In addition to featuring authors and selling books, they have a complete listing of African-American Bookstores and the largest list of African-American Book Clubs on the Internet. The Literary Freedom Project is Mosaic's not-for-profit arts organization, empowering communities of color through literature, creative thinking, and independent media.

PMA-online.org

Publishers Marketing Association (PMA) is a trade association of independent publishers. Founded in 1983, it serves book, audio, and video publishers located in the United States and around the world.

Its mission is to advance the professional interests of independent publishers. To this end, PMA provides cooperative marketing programs, education and advocacy within the publishing industry.

Publishers.org

This site contains a lot of information about book publishing. The Association of American Publishers, Inc. is noted as being the principal trade association of the book publishing industry.

Members have published all types of fiction and non-fiction. This site contains membership info as well as book publishing links. Chock full of information, including a link to the U.S. Copyright office.

Spawn.org

For editors and other publishing staff, this site provides info on writing, editing and publishing books. Also a membership available and important details on special events and meetings.

Timbooktu.com

This site offers stories, poetry and essays with an "African-American flavor", with an editor's message, and other links. Its helpful attribute is a link to other black websites.

But this site is unique in that it is a non-paying website for essayist, poets and writers to publish their works on the web. Work must have an afro-centric nature to it.

Visit this site for submission guidelines. If your work is not acceptable, the editor may contact you regarding revisions.

Writersandpoets.com

Earl Cox & Associates offers over 20 years of sales and marketing experience to book publishers that wish to sell books to the African American marketplace. They use a combination of grass roots promotion and highly visible events to generate sales and interest in your publishing program. All promotions are custom tailored to meet the needs of the individual.

Self-Publishing Online Resources

These are Companies that specifically offer "self-publishing" service options:

AmberBooks.com/QualityPress.html

With Quality Press, Arizona's personalized Self-Publishing program, you write the manuscript and Quality Press brings your book to fruition. For a one-time book-packaging fee Quality Press will coordinate your book project. Then, once you have paid your initial design, production and printing costs, you will receive the finished product within 6-8 weeks.

Quality Press has a top-notch design team with more than twenty-five years combined of Publishing, Promotion, Publicity & Marketing experience in all types and categories of books. We work with your theme to produce the most visual and marketable product for your success, including the size, colors, design and the title of your book. Design costs vary, according to the Cover style, Page Count and Size of the Book. Once the Company evaluates your basic self-publishing needs, they will have a specific print quote for you. They work with you to select the best printing house, paper stock and cover stock; and the best shipping options.

After a brief consultation, Quality Press will be able to determine your basic publishing needs; and upon reviewing your manuscript, they will furnish you with total production and printing fee estimates. Quality Press is the Self-Publishing Division of Amber Communications Group, Inc. The can be contacted at qualitypressaz@aol.com or 480-283-1098.

Iuniverse.com
This site provides publishing services while offering you total control and wide distribution, supported by their marketing resources. They have a variety of publishing programs that can get you started for minimal costs (You can get as few as 5 start-up books). Iuniverse also provides services, including a generous royalty and publishing time of less than 90 days.

Selfpublishedbooks.com
Founded in 1998 by Earl Cox, former African-American Books Sales Manager and National Accounts Manager for John Wiley & Sons, Publishers, Self published Books.com helps unpublished authors get their professionally edited manuscripts published, publicized and distributed worldwide.

Vantagepress.com
This is a subsidy book publisher. After paying them a fee which varies on your type of work, you will receive 40% on average they receive 20%. For an additional service fee, they offer a comprehensive marketing program, which lets you relax, while they promote your book.

Xlibris.com
Here they help you create your book, then print copies on-demand for your readers. Also allows you to keep all the rights to your work. They have a complete set of marketing tools for your convenience. You can talk to a publishing associate for assistance at 1-888-795-4274.

On-line eBook Resources

Adobe.com

Adobe ePaper® Solutions, you may take text files, paper documents, or Web sites, and can convert them to Adobe Portable Document Format (PDF) files with the original appearance preserved. Do collaborative markups, create searchable libraries, or electronically publish any type of document—ePaper Solutions will help you communicate more easily and effectively. PDF files are also a popular format for eBook readers.

EBookNet.com

EBookNet is your source for electronic books and electronic publishing: hardware, software and content. eBookNet covers eBooks, digital tablets, electronic readers, electronic publishing, news, hardware reviews, and forums.

Fatbrain.com

Fatbrain's eMatter lets individuals and companies publish and securely sell their work in digital format and receive a royalty on every copy sold. eMatter starts with authors uploading their original content in Microsoft Word, Adobe PDF, Postscript or ASCII text formats. Fatbrain.com secures those files in an encrypted Adobe PDF format. People can buy eMatter alone or with books, training materials and documents. Once purchased, eMatter is downloaded and secured to an individual's computer. People can read or print eMatter at any time with no strings attached.

Mesaview.com

MesaView's services allow customers to distribute their content to customers in multiple eBook Formats

Mightywords.com

(Fatbrain.com's new digital content marketplace) Once you register to publish and purchase eMatter, uploading your individual documents takes about five minutes a piece. All you do is enter information about your document, set your price, and upload your file. You maintain full editorial control and own the copyright. Mightywords takes a 50% commission (you set the price) and charges a $1.00 per month "storage fee".

Netlibrary.com

NetLibrary offers the world's largest library of eBooks. You may read eBooks online, search through them instantly and even "borrow" them.

Appendix B
Important Publishing Industry Contacts

African-American Bookstores

Black Classics - Books & Gifts
2206-D Airport Blvd.
Westwood Square
Mobile, AL 36606
Phone: 334-476-1060
Fax: 334-476-4642
Contact: Adline Clarke

Campus Bookstore
1013 Old Montgomery Road
Tuskegee Institute, AL 36088-1611

Lodestar Books
2020 - 11th Avenue South
Birmingham, AL 35205

Mahogany Books & Gifts
37 Western Hills Mall
Fairfield, AL 35064

Roots & Wings: A Cultural Bookplace
1345 Carter Hill Rd.
Montgomery, AL 36106-1421
(334) 262-1700
(334) 262-8498 (fax)
Contact: Gwen Boyd

Paradise Book Store
9008 N. 99th Avenue, #6
Peoria, AZ 85345
Contact: Joe Mercer
(623) 974-1748
jmer1748@juno.com

Pyramid
The Museum Center
500 East Markham, Suite 110
Little Rock, AR 72201
(501) 372-5824
Fax (501) 372-7133
Contact: Traci L. McKinley
pyramid@aristotle.net

Africa Enterprises
707 E. Broadway
W. Memphis, AR 72301
501-735-1212
Contact: Shabaka or Carol

The African Book Mart
2440 Durant Ave
Berkeley, CA 94704-1611
510-843-3088

African Heritage Books & Gifts
5191 3rd Street
San Francisco, CA 94124
Contact: Johnicon George

African Marketplace
2560 W. 54th Street
Los Angeles, CA 90043

Alkebulan Books
1757 Alcatraz Ave
510-653 8754
Berkeley, CA

Black Spring Books
503 Georgia Street
Vallejo, CA 94589
Contact: Jerry Thompson
(707) 556-9766

The Book House Cafe
Black Gay, Lesbian Transgender Books
484 Lakepark Ave #1
Oakland, CA 94610
(510) 268-0646
tbhcafe@pacbell.net

Books In Color
5444 Watt Avenue, Suite 900B
North Highlands, CA 95660
916 334-3026
Contact: Sherri

Bright Lights Bookstore
8461 S. Van Ness Ave.
Inglewood, CA 90305
(213) 971-1296
(805) 583-0207 (fax)
Contact: Michael McAllen

Carol's Books & Things
5964 S. Land Park Dr.
Sacramento, CA 95822

Marcus Books
1712 Filmore Street
San Francisco, CA 94115
(415) 346-4222
(415) 931-1536 (Fax)
Contact: Tamiko

A Different Booklist
746 Bathurst St.
Toronto, Canada
(416) 538-0889
Contact: Wesley Crichlow

Asiatic the Soul of Black Folks
544B St. Clair Avenue West
Toronto, Ontario
Canada M6C 1A5
416 838-5621

Burke's Books & Picture Framing
873 St. Clair Ave,
West Toronto, Ontario, M6C 1C4
Canada
(Toll Free) 877 276-3879
(416) 655-5366
(416) 656-9403 (fax)
burkesbooks@sprint.ca
Contact: Sam or Rita Burke

Knowledge Bookstore
18 Queen Street West
Brampton, Ontario
L6X 1A1 Canada
Tel 905-459-9875

Stouffville Book Connection Inc
6601 Main St. E
Stouffville Ontario, Canada
L4A 6A9
905 640 2907

Black And Read
7821 Wadsworth Blvd
Arvada, CO 80003-2107
303-467-3236

Hue-Man Experience
911 Park Ave. W.
Denver, CO 80205
(303) 293-2665
(303) 293-0046 (fax)

Black Books Galore, Inc.
65 High Ridge Rd., #407
Stamford, CT 06905-3806
(203) 359-6925
Contact: Toni Parker

Blackprint Heritage Gallery
162 Edgewood Ave
New Haven, CT 06511-4522
203-782-2159

Dygnyti Books
828 Dixwell Avenue
Hamden, CT 06514
(203) 776-9061
Email: dixwell@aol.com

EDEN Books
680 Blue Hills Avenue
P.O. Box 4338
Hartford, CT 06147-4338
(860) 568-9236
(860) 568-1213 (fax)
Contact: Yolanda Allen

Reflections Bookstore
37 Wintonbury Mall
Bloomfield, CT 06002
(860) 726-9155
(860) 726-9157 (Fax)
Contact: Pearline G. Hawkins

Drum and Spear Books
556 Varnum Street, N.W.
Washington, DC
202-722-4758
Contact: Gigi Roane

Howard University Bookstore
2225 Georgia Avenue, NW
Washington, DC 20059
(202) 238-2640 phone
(202) 986-1981 fax
Contact: Adrienne Mallard

Martin Luther King Library
901 G St NW
Washington, DC 200014599
(202) 727-1117
(202) 727-1129 (fax)
Contact: Coordinator of Adult Services

Sankofa Video and Bookstore
2714 Georgia Ave.,NW
Washington,DC 20001
(800) 524-3895
(202)-234-4755
fax 202-234-5735
e-mail sankofa@cais.com

Sisterspace and Books
1515 U Street, N.W.
Washington, D.C. 20009
(202) 332-3433
(202) 986-7092 (fax)
sistersp@erols.com

Yawa Books
2206 18th St. NW
Washington, DC 20009-1813
(202) 483-6805
Contact: Magaji Bukar

Haneef's Bookstore and Mosi Art
Gallery
911 N. Orange Street
Wilmington, DE 19801
(302) 656-4193
hanefBkst1@aol.com

African American Heritage Book
515 Northwood Rd; West
Palm Beach, FL 33407-5817
561-835-3551

African Bookstore
3600 W Broward Blvd
Fort Lauderdale, FL 33312-1014
954-584-0460

Amen-Ra's Bookstore and Gallery
1326 S. Adams Street
Tallahassee, FL 32304
(850) 681-6228

Books For Thought, Inc.
10910 N. 56th Street
Terrace Village Plaza
Tampa, FL 33617
(813) 988-6363
(813) 988-6866 (fax)
Contact: Felecia A. Wintons

Ethnic Elegance
9501Arlington Expressway
Jacksonville, FL 32225
(904) 725-0595
Contact: Reba Johnson

HBDC Bookstore @ Edward Waters
College
1601 Kings Road
Jacksonville, FL 32209
904-366-3707
Contact: Dorothy Hughes

Heritage Bookstore and More, Inc.
2219 Fowler Ave.
Fort Myers, FL 33901
Phone: 239.337.1558
Fax: 239.337-7398
contact: Maleta McPherson

Irmine's Books
PO Box 245342
Pembroke Pines, FL 33024
books@irmines.com

Love Christian Book Store
1968 Bruton Boulevard
Orlando, FL 32805

Montsho BookFairs, Etc., Inc.
2009 West Central Boulevard
Orlando, Florida 32805
407 648-8881
407 293-9408 (fax)
montshobks@aol.com
Contact: Jackie Perkins, CEO

Nefertiti's Books and Gifts
7640 Lem Turner Boulevard
Jacksonville, FL 32208
(904) 766-3630
Contact: Cathy and Naseem Maat

Pyramid Books
544-2 Gateway Blvd.
Boynton Beach, FL. 33535
(561)731-4422 (fax)
(561)731-0202

African Spectrum Book Store
Clarkston, Ga.
(770) 496-1140

Afro Books
871 Abernathy Blvd.,
Atlanta, GA

Celebrate
1015 Patina Pt.
Peachtree City, GA 30269-4013
(404) 486-1338
Contact: Sandra Napper

The Crowning Seat of Wisdom, Inc.
c\o Jeryl Muhammad
1130 Jackson Street
Madison, GA 30650
(fax) 706-342-8662
(email) broblack@msn.com

Freedom Now Bookstore
2118 Candler Road
Decatur, Georgia 30032
404-288-9880

Medu Bookstore
2841 Greenbriar Parkway, SW
Atlanta, GA 30331
(404) 346-3263

Mt. Zion Kid's Village
Little Angels Children's Bookstore
7175 Mt. Zion Blvd.
Jonesboro, GA 30236
678-479-3040

Mutana Afrikan Warehouse
1388 Abernathy Blvd, SW
Atlanta, GA 30310
404-753-5252
mutana@bellsouth.net

Nubian Bookstore
2449 Southlake Mall
Morrow, GA 30260
(678) 422-6120

The Reading Room Bookstore
56 Marietta Street NW
Atlanta, GA 30303
404.523.3241
404.523.3405 (fax)
bookvibes@aol.com

The Shrine of the Black Madonna
946 R. D. Abernathy Blvd., SW
Atlanta, GA 30130

Soul Source Bookstore
118 James P. Brawley Dr., S.W.
Atlanta, GA 30314
404-577-1346

The Tree of Life Bookstore of Harlem
1701 M.L. King Drive SW
Atlanta, GA 30314-2227
(404) 753-5700 (also fax#)
DrKanya@webtv.net

Two Friends Bookstore
598 Cascade Rd.
Atlanta, GA 30310
(404) 758-7711
(404) 753-0102 (fax)
Contact: Renecia Glass

Afri-Ware Inc.
948 Lake Str.
Oak Park, IL 60301
(708) 524-8398
(708) 524-8397(fax)
Contact: Jill Bunton
Afriware@aol.com

African American Images Inc
1909 W 95th St
Chicago, IL 60643-1105
312-445-0322

African By Nature
PO Box 257515
Chicago, IL 60625
Fax (773) 761-7838
sales@africanbynature.com

Afrocentric Book Store
234 S. Wabash Ave.
Chicago, IL 60604-2304
(312) 939-1956
Contact: Desiree Sanders

Black Expression Book Source
9500 5 Western Ave
Evergreen Park, IL 60805-2800
708-424-4338

Cultural Bookstore
100 W. Randolph
Second Level
Chicago, IL 60601
(312) 214-1314
(312) 214-1315 fax

The Epicenter Bookshop-UIC
750 S. Halsted St., #M-C048
Chicago, IL 60607-7008
(312) 413-5540
(312) 413-5526 (fax)
Contact Viktor Gliozeris

The Living Word Bookstore
3512 S. King Drive
Chicago, IL 60653
(312) 225-7500
Fitz Barclay

Reading Room Bookstore Global
Greetings International Gift Gallery
406 Main Street
Lafayette IN 47901
765-423-2604
email: globalgr2@hotmail.com

X-pression Bookstore & Gallery
970 Ft. Wayne Ave. #B
Indianapolis, IN 46202
317 264 1866
Contact: Donna Stokes-Lucas
112 S. State Street
Chicago, IL 60603

African American Gifts & Books
2219 E 13th St N
Wichita, KS 67214-1929
316-263-4742

Nimde Books
2200 W. Chestnut Street
Louisville, KY 40211

Community Book Center
217 N. Broad St.
New Orleans, LA 70119
phone: 504-822-BOOK(2665)
fax: 504-822-3947
contact: Vera Warren-Williams

The Black Library
325 Huntington Ave, Suite 83
Boston, MA 02115
Phone (617) 442-2400
Fax (617) 445-7514

Black Orchid Books
105 Columbia St
Maiden, MA 02148-3017
617-324-0404

Cultural Collections
730 Belmont Street
Brockton, MA 02301
(508) 580-1055
(508) 580-5197 (fax)
Contact: Juliet Armstrong

Jamaicaway Books & Gifts
676 Centre St.
Jamaica Plain, MA 02130
(617) 983-3204
(617) 983-2753
Contact: Rosalyn Elder

A Nubian Notion
41-47 Warren Street
Roxbury, MA 02119
Contact: Yvonne

African American Books and Publishing
2313 W Lafayette Ave
Baltimore, MD 21216-4817
410-945-8429

Arawak Books
3414 Hamilton St.
Hyattsville, MD 20783
301-277-9200

Ascension Books
5490 Cedar Lane, Ste. B3
Columbia, MD 21044
(301) 596-1669
Contact: Ken Williams
ascension-books@usa.net

Black By Popular Demand
5711 Ager Rd
Hyattsville, MD 20782-2602
301-559-8795

Everyone's Place
African Cultural Center
1380 W. North Avenue
Baltimore, MD 21217
410-728-0877

Karibu Books
3500 E. West Hwy.
Hyattsville, MD 20782-1916
(301) 559-1140
Contact: Brother Simba

MasterWorks Books
2703 Curry Drive
Adelphi, MD 20783
(301) 422-2168
(301) 422-1289 (fax)
Contact: William Coleman

Peek-A-Boo Books II
Wheaton Mall
11160 Veirs Mill Road
Wheaton, MD 20902
(301) 933-5312
Email: Pabbooks2@yahoo.com
Owners: Brian K. Jordan and
Marlon Green

Sepia, Sand, & Sable
6796 Reistersttown Rd,
Baltimore, MD 21215
(410) 318-8698

Sibanye
4031 Rogers Avenue,
Baltimore, MD 21215
(410) 542-0193
410-466-8924 fax
SIBANYEINC@aol.com

The Black Library
325 Huntington Ave, Suite 83
Boston, MA 02115
Phone (617) 442-2400
Fax (617) 445-7514

Black Orchid Books
105 Columbia St
Maiden, MA 02148-3017
617-324-0404

Cultural Collections
730 Belmont Street
Brockton, MA 02301
(508) 580-1055
(508) 580-5197 (fax)
Contact: Juliet Armstrong

Apple Book Center
7900 W. Outer Drive
Detroit, MI 48235
(313) 255-5221
(313) 255-5230 (fax)
Apple001@aol.com

B.T.S. Unlimited Books
19309 Greenfield Road
Detroit, MI 48235
phone 313-835-9094
contact: Jalani

Forewords Books & Gifts
Located in Originations Gallery
1671 Plymouth Road
Ann Arbor, MI 48105
(734) 662-9197
Contact: Carol or Floyd Jackson

LaCeter's Book Service
16345 Melrose St.
Southfield, MI 48075
(810) 569-5613
Contact: Sheila Gaddie

Mahogany Books
15768 Biltmore
Detroit, Ml 48227-1558
(313) 273-4479
Contact: Teresa Colquitt

The School House
19363 Livernois Avenue
Detroit, MI 48221
(313) 342-1261
(313) 342-0188 (fax)
Contact: Alan Wilder

Shrine of the Black Madonna
Book Store and Cutural Center
13535 Livernois Ave
Detroit, MI 48238
313-491-0777

The Truth Bookstore
Northland Mall #476
21500 Northwestern Highway
Southfield, MI 48075
phone 248-557-4824
contact: Nefertiti

Truth Boutique & Bookstore
Eastland Mall #823
18000 Vernier
Harper Woods, MI 48225
phone 313-371-2225
contact: Ajamu

Faith To Faith Books
1304 E. Lake St.
Minneapolis, MN 55411

The Presence of Africans In the Bible
Book Center
1012 - 26Th Av. N.,
Minneapolis, MN.. 55411
612-521-5570
612-521-5581 (fax)
contact: Leon Wallace Jr.

Uhuru Books
2917 Lyndale Ave S..
Minneapolis, MN 55407
(612) 721-7113
(612) 721-3128 (fax)

The Heritage Center
1414 Washington Street
Vicksburg, MS 39180
(601) 629-9010 (phone
(601) 629-9290 (fax)
HeritageCt@aol.com (e-mail)
Contact: Ezell McDonald

Too-No Books Etc.
PO Box 8203
Moss Point, MS 39562
(228) 474-7248
Contact: Deborah Washington

Afrocentric Books & Cafe
6172 Delmar
St. Louis, MO 63112
(314) 721-8550
Fax (314)725-1717
e-mail: Afrocentric@prodigy.net

Aframerican Book Store
3226 Lake St,
Omaha, Ne 68111.
402-455-9200

African American Book Store
216 1st St
Hackensack, NJ 07601-2400
201-343-0277

African Echoes Inc
PO BOX 6617
Somerset, NJ 08875-6617
Phone:(732) 246-1347
Fax: (732) 246-0629

African House Institute of Learning
505 Martin Luther King Jr. Dr
Jersey City, NJ 07304-2307
201-433-0191

BCA Books
P.O. Box 422
Cranbury, NJ 08512
(609) 275-1078
(609) 936-1299 (fax)
Catalog sales
(800) 995-0064
Contact: Monique or Martin
bcabooks@home.com

Black Pearl Books Plus
P.O. Box 5688
Englewood, NJ 07631-5688
(201) 568-0919
(201) 568-0919 (fax)
Contact: Arlena Ryland

Books 'n Things
Cross Keys Plaza
3501 Route 42
Turnersville, NJ 08080
856-740-2395

Crescent Office Store
494 Main Street
East Orange, NJ 07018
Phone: 973-414-6333
Fax: 973-678-8402
email: ihsannwk@aol.com
Contact: Abu Jamal James

Imoya Treasures, Inc
1465 Irving Street
Rahway, NJ 07065
Phone:732-388-4955
Fax:208-246-7796

Kujichagulia Book Store
150-154 Ellison Street
Paterson, New Jersey 07505
(973) 278-0919
Contact: Darlene Morris or
Jacqueline Smith

Mind & Soul Bookstore, Inc.
449 S. Broad St.
Trenton, NJ 08611
(609) 695-6606
Fax: (609) 695-2225
email: mindandsoul@email.msn.com

Netu Khisa Books and Gifts
131-133 South Orange Ave.
South Orange, NJ 07079
(973) 761-5669

Ourstory Books & Gifts
1318 South Ave
Plainfield, NJ 07062

Sacred Thoughts Bookstore
Newport Center Mall
Jersey City, NJ 07310
201/418-0100

Serengeti Plains
615 Bloomfield Avenue
Montclair, New Jersey 07042
(973) 783.2828
(973) 783.2886 fax

Tunde Dada House of Africa
356 Main Street
Orange, NJ 07050
(973) 673-4446
Fax (973) 673-4581

Tunde Dada House of Africa
Woodbridge Mall
Lower Level- Fortunoff Wing
337 Woodbridge Center Drive
Woodbridge, NJ 07095
(732) 636-0878

Yehudah Inc.
P.O. Box 1053
Teaneck, NJ 07666

A & B Distributors
146 Lawrence St.
Brooklyn NY 11217
718-596-0872

African Artisans
1211 Grand Ave
Baldwin, NY 11510-1115
516-481-5642

Black Mind Book Boutique
610 New York Ave
Brooklyn, NY 11203-1509
718-774-5800

Brooklyn MVP
Music and Book Store
818B Nostrand Ave.
(bet. E. Pkwy & Lincoln Pl.)
Brooklyn, NY 11216
718.774.3300
www.urbanbookstore.com

Brooklyn MVP
Music and Book Store
1624 Bedford Ave.
(bet. Carroll & Crown)
Brooklyn, NY 11225
718.771.7100
www.urbanbookstore.com

D & J Book Distributors
229-21B Merrick Blvd.
Laurelton, NY 11413
(718) 949-5400
(718) 949-6161 (fax)

DARE Books & Educational
Supplies
33 Lafayette Ave.
Brooklyn, NY 11217
(718) 625-4651
Contact: Desmond A. Reid

DeesBookNook Distributors
109-10 Liberty Avenue, #34A
So. Richmond Hills, NY 11419
Phone: 718-845-7413
Fax: 718-845-7420
Contact: Dee Stafford

House of Isis
236 / 5B West 135th St
New York, NY 10030
(212) 862-1026

HueMan Books
2319 Frederick Douglas Blvd
New York, NY 10027
(212) 885-7400
(212) 885-1071
huemanrdr@aol.com
Contact: Clara Villarosa

Langston Hughes Community Library
and Cultural Center
102-09 Northern Boulevard
Corona, NY 11368
718 651-1100 and 718 651-7116

Liberation Bookstore
421 Malcolm X Blvd.
New York, NY 10027
(212) 281-4615

Mood Makers Books & Art Gallery
Village Gate Square
274 N. Goodman St.
Rochester, NY 14807
716) 271-7010
716) 271-2313 (fax)
Contact: Curtis Rivers

Music on Myrtle
405 Myrtle Ave.
(bet. Vanderbilt & Clinton)
Brooklyn, NY 11205
Mon-Sat. 11am-8pm
Sun. Noon-6pm
718.596.MOMS (6667)
www.musiconmyrtyle.com

Nubian Heritage
560 Fulton St.
Brooklyn, NY 11217
(718) 797-4400
(718) 797-2420 (fax)
Email: trust@nubianheritage.com
Contact: Trust Graham

Our Black Heritage
2295 Adam Clayon Powell Blvd
New York, NY 10031
(917) 507-3133

Rainbow Books & Blooms
2016 Crompond Road
Yorktown Heights, N.Y. 10598
Phone: 914-243-3634
Fax: 914-243-3629
Contact: Anice Stephens

Revolution Books
9 West 19th St
New York, NY 10011
(212) 691-3345

The Schomburg Center for Research
Into Black Culture
(Gift Shop)
515 Malcolm X Blvd.
New York, NY 10037-1801
(212) 491-2200

Sisters Uptown Bookstore
1942 Amsterdam Ave
New York, NY 10032
(212) 862-0731

The Studio Museum of Harlem
(Gift Shop)
144 West 125th St.
New York, NY 10027
(212) 864-4500

Tunde Dada House of Africa
Green Acres Mall
Second Level- Sears Wing
2049 Green Acres Mall
Valley Stream, NY 11581
(516) 825-5601

Zawadi Gift Shop
519 Atlantic Ave. (bet 3rd & 4th Ave.'s)
Brooklyn, NY 11217
(718) 624-7822
(718) 624-6659 (fax)

Blacknificent Books & More
2011 Poole Rd
Raleigh, NC 27610
919-250-9110

Heritage House
901 S. Kings Drive
Charlotte, NC 28204
704-344-9695
Mon. - Sat. 10-6

King Solomon's Children's Enterprise
1308 Thurmond St.
Winston-Salem, NC 27105-5731
(910) 723-7706
Contact: Albert Thombs

The Know Bookstore
2520 Fayetteville St.
Durham, NC 27707

Special Occasions
112 N. Martin Luther King Jr. Dr.
Winston-Salem, NC 27101-4407
(919) 724-0334
Contact: E.L. McCarter

W & W African American Art
Specializing in Books & Gift Items, Etc.
417 Cross Creek Mall
Fayetteville, NC 28303
(910) 868-7090

The African Book Shelf
1324Q Euclid Ave
Cleveland, OH 44112-4524
216-681-6511

African & Islamic Books Plus
3752 Lee Rd
Cleveland, OH 44128-1410
216-561-5000

Baruti-Ba Books
PO Box 1684
Dayton OH 45401
Contact: Kevin Tucker

Black Art Plus
3269 W. Siebenthaler Avenue,
Dayton, OH 45406
937-277-8842

Brighter Day Books & Gifts
5941 Hamilton Ave.
Cincinnati, OH 45224-3045
(513) 542-6764
Contact: Dolores Rolland

A Cultural Exchange
12621 Larchmere Blvd.
Cleveland, OH 44120-1109
(216) 229-8300
(216) 795-5302 (fax)
Contact: Lloyd McHamm

Lady Grace Bookshop & Gifts
P. O. Box 1651
1044 Cleveland Rd
Sandusky, OH 44870
email: ladygrace@sanduskyoh.com
or harmony31@aol.com
419-621-1991
1-888-541-2143
fax 419-625-1539

People's Books & Gifts
1528 S. Yellowsprings Street
Springfield, OH 45506

Timbuktu
5508 Superior Avenue
Cleveland, OH 44103
(216) 391-4740

Ujamaa Book Store
1511 E. Livingston Avenue
Columbus, Ohio 43205
(614) 258-4633 Fax
(614) 258-2082

Paperback Connection
5120 N. Classen Blvd.
Oklahoma City, OK
(405) 789-2494
Contact: Vanessa

Sweet Spirit Bookstore & Gift Shop
4621 N.E. 23rd Street
Oklahoma City, Oklahoma 73121
(405) 427-7521
Fax: (405) 424-4122
E-mail: 3379joy@msn.com

Reflections Coffee and Bookstore
Walnut Park Retail Center
446 NE Killingsworth Street
Portland, Oregon 97211
503.288.6942

Basic Black Books
Gallery One - Mall Level
9th & Market St
Philadelphia, PA 19107
(215) 922-4417
(215) 922-7784
Contact: Lecia

Gene's Books
King of Prussia Plaza
King of Prussia, PA 19406-3149
610) 265-6210
610) 265-6260 (fax)
Contact Rashena Wilson

Hakim's Bookstore and Gift Shop
210 S 52nd St
Phila Pa 19139
215-474-9495
Fax 215-748-5414

Know Thyself
Bookstore and Cultural
Development Center
528 S. 52nd St.
Philadelphia, PA 19143
(215) 748-2278
Contact: Brother Deke

Ligorius Bookstore Inc
Cheltenham Square Mall Shopping Ctr
Philadelphia, Pa 19150
(215) 549-0995

Books in the Black
228 Somerset Drive
Columbia, SC 29223
(803) 699-9252
Contact: Barbara Preston

Dorothea's African-American Books
and Gifts
5410-D Two Notch Road
Columbia, SC 39204
803-782-9833

PowerHouse Books
1424 Horreil Hill Rd.
Hopkins, SC 29061

(803) 785-3032
(803) 785-3065 (fax)
Contact Lovera W. Robertson

Off The Shelf African American Books
903 Elmwood Ave.
Suite C.
Columbia, SC 29201
(803)731-5341
Contact: Charlene Ruff

TDIR Books
6920 North Main Street
Columbia, SC 29203
(803) 754-5911
Toll Free: (888) 246-8211
(803) 754-4922 (fax)

African American Gift Gallery
114 Carr St.
Knoxville,TN 37919
(423) 584-1320
Contact: Leslie Valentine

Alkebu-Lan Images Bookstore &
Gift Shop
2721 Jefferson Street
Nashville, Tennessee 37208
Phone: (615) 321-4111
Fax: (615) 321-4110

Cultural Expressions Bookstore
659 Providence Blvd
Clarksville, TN 37042
931-572-1001

Ethnic Image Books & More
3023 Nolensville Pike #C
Nashville TN 37211
615/832-1101
ethnicimagebooks@aol.com

Sidewalk University
2287 Union Avenue
Memphis, TN 38104
Phone: (901) 722-2110
Fax: (901) 722-2112

CushCity
13559 Bammel N. Houston Rd.
Houston, TX 77066
Phone: (281) 444-4265
Fax: 281-583-9534
Contact: Gwen Richardson
www.cushcity.com

Babatunde & Yetunde
1102 W. Jaspter Rd.
Killeen, TX 76541
(877) 556-2816
www.uor@killeen.com

The Black Bookworm
605 E Berry St
Fort Worth, TX 76110-4300
817-923-9661

The Black Bookworm
2300 Ridgeview St.
Fort Worth, TX 76119-3125
817-535-0366

Black Images Book Bazaar
230 Wynnewood Village
PO Box 41059
Dallas, TX 75224
(214) 943-0142
(214) 941-3932 (fax)
Contact: Derrick Rodgers

Black Book Discounters
4720 La Branch
Houston, Texas 77004
713 520-5188

Exhale African American Books & Gifts
5555 New Territory Blvd # 9102
Sugar Land, Texas77478
281-240-2962
Twoxhale@aol.com

Jokae's African-American Books+
3917 W. Camp Wisdom
Suite #107
Dallas, TX 75237
(972) 283-0558
(800) 749-7225
(972) 283-0559(fax)

MainStreet Books
4201 Main St
Houston, TX 77002
(713) 527-2289

Nu World of Books
3250 Washington Blvd.
Beaumont, TX 77705
(409) 842-1412

Out of Africa
Windsor Park Mall
7900 IH 35 N.
San Antonio, TX 78218
(210) 599-7830
Contact: Eromosele Alegbe

Shrine of the Black Madonna
5309 M.L.K. King
Houston, TX 77021
(713) 645-1071
(713) 645-2469 (fax)

Tricia's Books N' Things
11975 Swords Creek
Houston, TX 77067

Under One Roof Afrikan American
Bookstore
1102 West Jasper Drive
Killeen, TX 76542
254-554-6553
email uor@killeen.com

Education Central
Sunny Isle Shopping Plaza
St. Croix, U.S. Virgin Islands

Sam Weller Books
254 S Main
Salt Lake City UT 84101
(801) 328-2586

Atlantic Bookpost
11654 Plaza America Drive #173
Reston, VA 20190-4700
703-638-6719
703-638-6842 Fax

Cultural Expression
P.O. Box 8464
Newport News, VA 23606-0464
(757) 826-0733
(757) 826-3512 (fax)
Contact: Charlotte Marie Callins

One Force Books
217 E. Clay Street
Richmond, VA 23219

Positive Vibes
6220 B Indian River Rd.
Virginia Beach, Va. 23464
(757) 523-1399

Words of Wisdom Books and Gifts
P.O. Box 4777
Norfolk, VA 23523
(757) 543-3362

Brother's Books
11443 Rainier Ave. S.
Seattle, WA 98178-3954
(206) 772-0330
(206) 772-7811 (fax)
Contact: Mary Lou

Carol's Essentials Ethnic Gifts and Books
1106 23rd Avenue
Seattle, WA 98122
(206) 322-9390
(206) 322-6351 (fax)
carolsessentials@email.msn.com

Life Enrichment Bookstore
8300 Rainier Avenue South
Seattle, WA 98118
(206) 722-7785
Vickie Williams

Black Swan Books & Coffee
765-G Woodlake Rd
Kohler, WI 53044-1321
414-458-4757

The Cultural Connection Bookstore
3424 W. Villard Ave.
Milwaukee, WI 53209-4710
(414)461-6160
(800) 462-6160
(414) 461-1788 (fax)
Contact: Frances Utsey

The Reader's Choice
1950 N. Dr. Martin Luther King Jr. Dr.
Milwaukee, WI 53212
(414) 265-2003
(414) 449-9476 (fax)
Contact Carla Allison

African-American Distributors

A & B Distributors
1000 Atlantic Avenue
Brooklyn, NY 11238
(718) 783-7808
Contact: Eric Gift

Afrikan World Books
2217 Penn Ave. Box 16447
Baltimore, MD 21217
(410) 728-0877
Contact: Brother Nati

Culture Plus Books
291 Livingston Street
Brooklyn, NY 11217
(718) 222-9309
Contact: Larry Cunningham

D & J Book Distributors
229-21B Merrick Boulevard
Laurelton, NY 11413
718-949-5400
718-949-6161
Contact: David Reeves

Distributors & Wholesalers

Book Buyer
Academic Books
5600 N. E.Hassalo St.
Portland, OR 97213
(503) 287-6657

Book Buyer, Catalog Dept.
Amazon.com
705 Fifth Ave. South
Seattle, WA 98104
(206) 266-3396
books-dept@amazon.com

Book Buyer
Baker & Taylor Books
P.O. Box 6885
Bridgewater, NJ 08807
(800) 775-2300

Asst. Buyer, Small Press Dept.
Barnes & Noble
122 Fifth Ave.
New york, NY 10011
(212) 633-3549

Purchasing
Blackwell's Book Services
100 University Court
Blackwood, NJ 08012
(800) 547-6426

Book Buyer
Book Wholesalers Inc.
1847 Mercer Road
Lexington, KY 40511
(800) 888-4478

Book Buyer
Brodart, Inc.
500 Arch St.
Williamsport, PA 17701
(800) 233-8467

Purchasing
Follett Library Resources
1340 Ridgeview Dr.
McHenry, Il 60050
(888) 511-5114

Book Buyer
Ingram Books
One Ingram Boulevard
LaVergne, TN 37086
(800) 937-8100

Book Buyer
Koens Book Distributors
10 Twosome Drive
Moorestown, NJ 08057
(800) 257-8481

Book Buyer
Last Gasp
777 Florida St.
San Francisco, CA 94110

Book Buyer
Midwest Library Services
11443 St. Charles Rock Road
Bridgeton, MO 63044
(314) 739-2999

Book Buyer
Partners Book Distributors
2325 Jarco Drive - P.O. Box 580
Holt, MI 48842
(800) 336-3137

Acquisitions Coordinator
Publishers Group West
1700 Fourth St.
Berkeley, CA 94710
(800) 788-3123

Book Buyer
Quality Books, Inc.
1003 West Pines Road
Oregon, IL 61061
(800) 323-4241

Book Buyer
Tower Books
2601 Delmonte
West Sacramento, CA 95691

Book Buyer
Unique Books
5010 Kemper Ave.
St. Louis, MO 63139
(314) 776-6695

Book Buyer
Yankee Book Peddler
999 Maple St.
Contoocook, NH 03229
(603) 746-3102

African-American Literary Agents

Janell Walden Agyeman
Marie Brown & Associates
990 NE 82nd Terrace
Miami, FL 33138-4116

Jacqueline Turner Banks
Banks Communications
7515 Bruno Way
Sacramento, CA 95828

Audra Barrett
Barrett Books
12138 Central Avenue, Suite 183
Mitchellville, MD 20721
(301) 627-2104
audra@barrettbooksagency.com

Marie Brown
Marie Brown & Associates
625 Broadway #902
New York, NY 10012

Faith Childs Literary Agency, Inc.
915 Broadway, Suite 1009
New York, NY 10010

Marlene Connor
Connor Literary Agency
2911 West 71st Street
Richfield, MN 55423

Crichton & Associates, Inc.
6940 Carroll Avenue
Takoma Park, MD 20912
Tel: 301-495-9663
Fax: 202-318-0050
Email: cricht1@aol.com
www.crichton-associates.com

Lisa Davis
Lisa Davis Literary Agency
301 1/2 Second Street
Jersey City, NJ 07302

J Lawrence Jordan
Lawrence Jordan Literary Agency
250 West 57th St., #1517
New York, NY 10107

John McGregor
JMG Books
199 Grand Avenue
Freeport, NY, 11520

Tanya McKinnon
c/o Mary Evans Inc.
242 E. 5th St.
New York, NY 10003
212-979-0880

Michael Phifer
PMM Literary Agency
2420 Hunter Ave Ste. 20
Bronx NY 10475
718-862-1575
mike-p@chesmaTv.com

Denise L. Stinson
33290 West Fourteen Mile Road #482
West Bloomfield, MI 48301

African American Magazines

A Time to Style Magazine
P.O. Box 244
New York, NY 10032
(914) 332-6406

American Legacy Magazine
60 Fifth Ave.
New York, NY 10011
(212) 620-2204

Black Beat Magazine
333 Seventh Ave
New York, NY 10001
(212) 780-3500

Black Elegance Magazine
1040 First Avenue
New York, NY 10022
(212) 439-1789

Black Enterprise
130 Fifth Ave.
New York, NY 10011-4399
(212) 242-8000

Black Issues Book Review
Empire State Building
350 Fifth Ave #1215
New York, NY 10118
(212) 947-5698

Black Men Magazine
210 Route 4 East
Paramus, NJ 07652-5116
(201) 843-4004

Black Voices.com
435 N. Michigan Ave. #Suite L2
Chicago, IL 60611
(312) 222-4228

BlackWebPortal.com
450 Shrewsbury Plaza - Suite 245
Shrewsbury, NJ 07702
Ph: (732) 918-8519
Fax: (732) 918-8519

Blackboard Times
5361 Refugee Road
Columbus, OH 43232
(614) 863-3946

Blac-Tress / Black Hair Care
1115 Broadway - 8th Floor
New York, NY 10010

Disilgold Publishing, Inc.
P.O. Box 652
Baychester Station, Bronx, NY 10469
(917) 757-1658

Diversity City Media
225 West 3rd Street
Suite #203
Long Beach, CA 90802
(562) 209-0616
info@diversitycity.com

Ebony Magazine
820 S. Michigan Ave.
Chicago, IL 60605
(312) 322-9200

Essence Magazine
1500 Broadway
New York, NY 10036
(212) 642-0600

Heart & Soul
1900 W Place NE
Washington, DC 20018-1211
(202) 608-2800

Hype Hair & Beauty
210 Route 4 East #401
Paramus, NJ 07652
(201) 843-4004

Jet Magazine
820 S. Michigan Ave.
Chicago, IL 60605
(312) 322-9200

Jive Magazine
C/O Dorchester Media LLC
333 Seventh Avenue - 11th Floor
New York, NY 10001
212-780-3500

Just For Black Men
210 Route 4 East #401
Paramus, NJ 07652
(201) 843-4004

The Kip Business Report
1916 Park Avenue #601
New York, NY 10037
(212) 961-0809

Mirror-Gibbs Publications
P.O. Box 6573
Oakland, CA 94603
(510) 409-9571

Latina Magazine
1500 Broadway - Ste 600
New York, NY 10036
(212) 642-0600

The Network Journal
139 Fulton St. Suite 407
New York, NY 10038
(212) 962-3791

Quarterly Black Review
9 West 126th St. - 2nd
New York, NY 10027
(212) 348-1681

Right On! Magazine
333 Seventh Ave.
New York, NY 10001
(212) 780-4823

Sophisticate's Black Hair Care
Magazine
875 North Michigan Ave. Ste 3434
Chicago, IL 60611
(312) 266-8680

Success Guide
FraserNet, Inc.
2940 Noble Road - Suite 1
Cleveland, OH 44121
Ph: (216) 691-6686
Fax: (216) 691-6685

Today's Black Woman
210 Route 4 East #401
Paramus, NJ 07652
(201) 843-4004

True Confessions Magazine
C/O Dorchester Media LLC
333 Seventh Avenue - 11th Floor
New York, NY 10001
212-780-3500

Upscale Magazine
600 Bronner Brothers Way SW
Atlanta, GA 30310
(404) 754-7467

Word Up!
210 Route 4 East
Paramus, NJ 07652-5116
(201) 843-4004

African American Newspapers

Arizona Informant
1746 E. Madison #2
Phoenix, AZ 85034
Ph: (602) 257-9300

Los Angeles Sentinel
3800 Crenshaw Blvd.
Los Angeles, CA 90008
Ph: (213) 299-3800
Fax: (213) 299-3896

Oakland Post
630 20th St.
Oakland, CA 94612
Ph: (510) 287-8200
Fax: (510) 763-9670

Washington Afro American
1612 14th Street NW
Washington, DC 20009
Ph: (202) 232-0080

Washington Informer
3117 MLK Jr. Ave. SE
Washington, DC 20032
Ph: (202) 561-4100
Fax: (202) 882-9817

The Washington Post
1150 15th St. NW
Washington, DC 20071
Ph: (202) 334-7881
Fax: (202) 544-7874

Washington Sun
830 Kennedy St. NW
Washington, DC 20011
Ph: (202) 882-1021

Jacksonville Advocate
1284 West 20th Street
Jacksonville, FL 32209-4302
Ph: (904) 764-4740
Fax: (904) 766-5542
JaxAdvocate@aol.com

Jacksonville Free Press
903 Edgewood Ave West
Jacksonville, FL 32208
Ph: (904) 634-1993
jfreepress@aol.com

The Atlanta Inquirer
P.O. Box 92367
Atlanta, GA 30314-0367
Ph: (404) 523-6086
news@theatlantainquirer.com

The Columbus Times
2230 Buena Vista Road
Columbus, GA 31907
Ph: (403) 324-2404

Atlanta Tribune
875 Old Roswell Rd, Suite C
Roswell, GA 30076
Ph: (404) 587-0501
plottier@mindspring.com

Chicago Defender
2400 S. Michigan Ave.
Chicago, IL 60616
Ph: (312) 225-2400
editorial@chicagodefender.com

Chicago Sun Times
401 N. Wabash - 4th Fl.
Chicago, IL 60611
Ph: (312) 321-2854
Fax: (312) 321-3027

Frost Illustrated
3121 South Calhoun St.
Fort Wayne, IN 46807
Ph: (260) 745-0552
frostnews@aol.com

Bay State Banner
23 Drydock Ave.
Boston, MA 02210
Ph: (617) 261-4600

Unity First Direct
189 Braeburn Road
East Longmeadow, MA 01028
Ph: (413) 734-6444
editors@unityfirst.com

Cape Verdean News
P.O. Box 3063
New Bedford, MA 02741
Ph: (509) 997-2300

Baltimore Afro American
2519 North Charles Street
Baltimore, MD 21218
Ph: (410) 554-8200
Fax: (410) 554-8213
willieg@afroam.org

Baltimore Times
2513 N. Charles St.
Baltimore, MD 21218
Ph: (410) 366-3900
Fax: (410) 243-1627
dwane@btimes.com

Michigan Chronicle
479 Ledyard St.
Detroit, MI 48201
Ph: (313) 963-5522
chronicle4@aol.com

Times Newspapers
P.O. Box 7258
Grand Rapids, MI 49510

The New Citizens Press Newspaper
P.O. Box 19006
Lansing, MI 48901
(517) 372-8466

Saint Louis Sentinel Newspaper
2900 North Market
St. Louis, MO 63106

St. Louis American
4242 Lindell Blvd.
St. Louis, MO 63108
Ph: (314) 533-8000
areid@stlamerican.com

St. Louis Argus
4595 MLK Drive
St. Louis, MO 63113
Ph: (314) 531-1323

African Sun Times
463 N. Arlington Ave. #17
East Orange, NJ 07017-3927
Ph: (212) 791-4073
Fax: (212) 791-0777
afrstime@aol.com

Afro Times
1195 Atlantic Ave.
Brooklyn, NY 11216
Ph: (718) 636-9500
Fax: (718) 857-9115
afrotimes@blackplanet.com

Caribbean Life
1733 Sheepshead Bay road
Brooklyn, NY 11235
Ph: (718) 769-4400
Fax: (718) 769-5048

Christian Times
1061 Atlantic Ave.
Brooklyn, NY 11238
(718) 638-5483

Daily Challenge
1195 Atlantic Ave.
Brooklyn, NY 11216
Ph: (718) 636-9500
Fax: (718) 857-9115

Buffalo Challenger
1303 Fillmore Ave.
Buffalo, NY 14211

New York Voice
175-61 Hillside Ave. #201
Jamaica, NY 11432
Ph: (718) 206-9866
Fax: (718) 206-9803

CARIB News
15 West 39th St.-13th floor
New York, NY 10018
Ph: (212) 944-1991
Fax: (212) 944-2089
caribnews@worldnet.att.net

Harlem News
P.O. Box 1775
New York, NY 10027
Ph: (212) 996-6006
Fax: (212) 996-6010
harlemnewsetc@aol.com

Kip Business Report
1916 Park Ave,. South #601
New York, NY 10037
Ph: (212) 690-1017
Fax: (212) 961-0815
kbr@kipcommunications.com

Network Journal
139 Fulton St. #407
New York, NY 10038
Ph: (212) 962-3791
Fax: (212) 962-3537

New York Beacon
12 East 33rd St.- 6th fl.
New York, NY 10016
Ph: (212) 213-8585
Fax: (212) 213-6291

NY Amsterdam News
2340 Frederick Douglas Blvd - 4th Fl.
New York, NY 10027
Ph: (212) 932-7400
Fax: (212) 932-7467

Columbus Post
172 East State St. - Suite 203
Columbus, OH 43215-4321
Ph: (614) 251-1722
Fax: (614) 251-1745

Philadelphia Tribune
520 South 16th St.
Philadelphia, PA 19146
Ph: (215) 893-4050
editorial@phila-tribune.com

The Tennessee Tribune
1501 Jefferson St.
Nashville, TN 37208
Ph: (615) 321-3268
Fax: (615) 321-0409
Tenn37208@aol.com

Houston Defender
P.O. Box 8005
Houston, TX 77288
Ph: (713) 663-7716

Book Publishers

Amber Communications Group, Inc.
1334 East Chandler Blvd - #5-D67
Phoenix, AZ 85048

Amistad Press/Harper Collins
10 East 53rd St.
New York, NY 10023

Arabesque / BET Books
1900 West Place NE - One BET Plaza
Washington, DC 20018

Artria Books
1230 Avenue of Americas
New York, NY 10020

Black Classic Press
4701-D Mt. Hope Drive
Baltimore, MD 21215

BET Books
850 Third Ave.
New York, NY 10022

Black Expressions Book Club
1271 Avenue of Americas - 3rd fl.
New York, NY 10020

Booksthatclick.com
1625 Nottingham Way
Mountainside, NJ 07092

Crown Publishing
1745 Broadway
New York, NY 10019

Doubleday/Harlem Moon Books
1745 Broadway
New York, NY 10019

FYOS Entertainment, LLC
P.O. Box 25216
Philadelphia, PA 19119

Genesis Press, Inc.
Court Square Towers, Suite 101
Columbus, MS 39705

Harper Collins Publishers
10 East 53rd St.
New York, NY 10022

Henry Holt & Company
115 West 18th St.
New York, NY 10011

Hilton Publishing Company, Inc.
P.O. Box 737
Roscoe, IL 61073

Howard University Press
2900 Van Ness St. NW
Washington, DC 20008

John Wiley & Sons, Inc.
111 River St.
Hoboken, NJ 07030

Johnson Publishing
820 S. Michigan Ave.
Chicago, IL 60605

Just Us Books
356 Glenwood Avenue East
Orange, NJ 07017

Kensington Publishing Corp.
850 Third Ave.
New York, NY 10022

One World/Ballantine
1745 Broadway
New York, NY 10019

Penguin Putnam, Inc.
375 Hudson St.
New York, NY 10014

Random House
1745 Broadway
New York, NY 10019

Red Sea Press / Africa World Press, Inc.
541 West Ingham Ave. Suite V
Trenton, NJ 08638

Seaburn Publishing
P.O. Box 030064
Elmont, NY 11003

Simon & Schuster
1230 Avenue of Americas
New York, NY 10020

St Martins Press
175 Fifth Avenue
New York, NY 10010

Strebor Books International
P.O. Box 1370
Bowie, MD 20718

Third World Press
7822 South Dobson
Chicago, IL 60619

Walk Worthy Press
33290 West Fourteen Mile Road
#482
West Bloomfield, MI 48322

William Morrow
1350 Ave of Americas
New York, NY 10249

Quality Press, the Self-Publishing Division of Amber Communications Group, Inc. (ACGI) has **thousands of contacts, available!!**

Mailing Labels or Lists that will help you reach your marketing goal.

Available to All Authors (Published/Self-Published and Aspiring) Who Want to Start or Expand Their Book Publishing Business.

With these resources you will be able to specifically **target your market**:

▼ African-American BOOKSTORES
▼ In-general BOOKSTORES
▼ African-American LIBRARY COLLECTION & ACQUISITIONS PERSONNEL
▼ In-general LIBRARY COLLECTIONS & ACQUISITIONS PERSONNEL
▼ African-American NEWSPAPER PUBLISHERS & EDITORS
▼ In general NEWSPAPER PUBLISHERS & EDITORS
▼ African-American NATIONAL MAGAZINE EDITORS
▼ In general NATIONAL MAGAZINE EDITORS
▼ Historically BLACK COLLEGES & BLACK COLLEGE BOOKSTORES
▼ FOUNDATIONS & ORGANIZATIONS
▼ URBAN RADIO STATION PROGRAM DIRECTORS & Talk Show Hosts
▼ BOOK PUBLISHERS & EDITORS
▼ DISTRIBUTORS / Wholesalers

For information and orders, call Terry: 480-283-1098 or Email: qualitypressaz@aol.com

Don't forget to ask Quality Press how you can promote your self-published book to more than 10,000 African-American retail, bookstore and library prospects by listing your book in ACGI's Nationally Distributed Catalogue.

If you are an author planning to Self-Publish your first book, we can guide you through the process. Contact Quality Press for your **FREE CONSULTATION** to evaluate your Basic Publishing Needs: 480-283-0991 or Email: qualitypressaz@aol.com

Appendix C
Successful Self-Published Authors Who Were Destined To Win

All of the famous authors in this section self-published their first book. With talent, dedication, and courage, you, too, can gain fame and fortune.

Kwame Alexander
As a poet, stage director, producer, editor and publisher, **Kwame Alexander** is a pivotal figure in the current renaissance of Black literature and performance. He holds a BA Degree in Psychology, English and Black Studies from Virginia Tech, where he studied for three years under the renowned poet Nikki Giovanni, and edited the student literary journal, Umoja.

Alexander is the Founder and CEO of Blackwords, Inc. an independent publishing house dedicated to providing publishing opportunities for the many talented literary voices of the Hip-Hop Generation.

Kwame is the also the author of several books of poetry: Survival in Motion (1993), *The Flow: New Black Poetry in Motion* (1994), *Just Us: Poems and Counterpoems* 1986-1995, which was awarded the 1996 international Black Book Award for Poetry, Kupenda: Love Poems (2002). He is also the co-editor of the best selling BlackWords title, *Tough Love* (1996), a collection of essays, poems and critical commentary from 26 writers on the life and death of slain "gangsta" rapper Tupac Shakur.

Alexander has been widely published and featured in newspapers and magazines including *Vibe Magazine, Source Magazine, Amsterdam News, Chicago Tribune* and *QBR: The Black Book Review.*

Kwame Alexander works and lives outside of Washington, DC.

Nikki Giovanni
Nikki Giovanni is the author of thirteen books of poetry including Love Poems, for which she received an NAACP Image Award, and The Selected Poems of Nikki Giovanni. Ms. Giovanni began her publishing career as a

self-published author, riding around with books in her trunk; and in 1970 she founded a publishing company called Niktom Limited.

An American poet, essayist, and children's writer, she is known for her writings about the experiences of black people, particularly women, living in American cities. Currently, her books are being published by William Morrow Publishing.

Many of Giovanni's earlier poems were collected in *The Selected Poems of Nikki Giovanni (1968-1995)*, published in 1996. Her later poems appear in such collections as *The Sun Is So Quiet* (1996), *Love Poems* (1997), *Blues for All Changes: New Poems*(1999), and *Quilting the Black-Eyed Pea: Poems and Not Quite Poems* (2002). Many of her children's poems are in *Ego Tripping and Other Poems for Young People* (1973). Her essays are collected in *Gemini* (1971), *Sacred Cows...and Other Edibles* (1988), and *Racism 101* (1994).

Other Major Works written by Ms. Giovanni include: *Black Feeling, Black Talk* (1968), *Black Judgement* (1968), *Gemini: An Extended Autobiographical Statement on My First Twenty-Five Years of Being a Black Poet* (1971), *Spin a Soft Black Song: Poems for Children* (1971) *My House, Ego-Tripping and Other Poems for Young People* (1973), *Vacation Time: Poems for Children (1980), Those Who Ride the Night Winds* (1983), *The Collected Poetry of Nikki Giovanni : 1968-1998* (2003).

Yolanda Cornelia "Nikki" Giovanni was born in Knoxville, Tennessee, and raised in Ohio. In 1960, she entered Fisk University, where she worked with the school's Writer's Workshop and edited the literary magazine. After receiving her Bachelor of Arts degree, she organized the Black Arts Festival in Cincinnati and then entered graduate school at the University of Pennsylvania.

Ms. Giovanni's honors include the NAACP Image Award for Literature in 1998, and the Langston Hughes award for Distinguished Contributions to Arts and Letters in 1996. Several magazines have named Giovanni Woman of the Year, including Essence, Mademoiselle, and Ladies Home Journal. She is currently Professor of English and Gloria D. Smith Professor of Black Studies at Virginia Tech.

E. Lynn Harris

Despite his literary focus on black, young, middle-class, urban professionals, E. Lynn Harris and his three younger sisters were raised by their single mother, who worked in an AT&T factory in Little Rock, Arkansas. He was 14 when he first met his father, who was killed the following year.

After graduating with honors from the University of Arkansas at Fayetteville in 1977, Harris went to work as a sales executive for IBM.

He quit his job as a computer salesman and used $25,000 of his own money to print Invisible Live, which in the wake of the ensuing frenzy was published as a Doubleday paperback in 1994 and quickly soared to number one on the Blackboard Bestseller List of African American titles. Since then, E. Lynn Harris has maintained a long-term relationship with his publisher Doubleday Books.

Just as I Am (1994), his second novel, made Harris the first male writer to have a number-one hardcover on the Blackboard list. His third novel, *And This Too Shall Pass* (1996), debuted on Blackboard at number one and spent nine weeks on the New York Times bestseller list. In 1996, *Just as I Am* received the Novel of the Year prize from Blackboard African American Bestsellers, Inc.

Other best-selling novels by E. Lynn Harris include: *What Becomes of the Brokenhearted* (2003, *A Love of My Own* (2002), *Any Way the Wind Blows* (2001), *Not a Day Goes By* (2000), *Abide With Me* (1999), and *If This World Were Mine* (1997)

William July

William July, II is an award winning author and lecturer popular for his candid approach to relationship and self-transformation issues of today. He has been featured and interviewed in the media across the country including: ABC, NBC, CBS, Fox, Newsday, Dallas Morning News, Ebony, Essence and Heart and Soul.

A former real estate broker, police officer and political aide, William July self-published his first best-selling version of *Brothers, Lust and Love* in 1996. He is now the author of four books on the Broadway/Random House Imprint, including the revision of his first best-seller, *Brothers, Lust and Love* (1998), *Understanding The Tin Man* (2001), *Men Can't Tell* (2003) and *Confessions of an Ex-Bachelor: How to Sift Through all the Game's Players to Find Mr. Right* (2003). He is currently at work on his next book.

In addition to speaking and writing, July is also active in his community. He's a writer in residence with the Writers In The Schools program, teaching creative writing to elementary school children. July also teaches a seminar course on publishing at the Houston Community College. He has been the recipient of several achievement awards and citations for outstanding community service.

Mr. July lives in Houston, Texas.

Haki Madhubuti

In 1973, Don Lee, a leader in the Black Arts Movement, changed his name to Haki Madhubuti. Born in Detroit, and having moved to Chicago after his mother's death, Madhubuti would sow the seeds that later led to his success. After graduation from high school, he was drafted into military service, where he used books as his escape. After his tour of duty, he returned to Chicago and immersed himself in the black arts world.

Madhubuti became apprentice and curator at the DuSable Museum of African History in 1963 and worked closely with Margaret Burroughs, a scholar of pan-African history. During the four years he spent at the museum with Burroughs, he had met some of the most prominent forces in the African American arts community, including Gwendolyn Brooks, who encouraged him to publish a collection of his poetry.

The result, *Think Black*, appeared in 1966 and was entirely self-published and self-distributed. It had been written in black dialect and slang and via Madhubuti's influence on the recording group, The Last Poets his poetry is a strong predecessor of the 90s music style called Rap.

After selling several hundred copies of *Think Black* within a week, Madhubuti realized that the dream of independent publishing—free from established corporate interests—could be attained. The following year, Madhubuti and two partners launched the Third World Press in the basement of his Chicago apartment with $400 and a mimeograph machine. In this humble setting, an institution was born.

Madhubuti attended several colleges in Chicago and graduate school at the University of Iowa (M.F.A., 1984). He taught at various colleges and universities, in 1984 becoming a faculty member at Chicago State University.

Madhubuti has published more than twenty-two books of essays and poetry and has become one of the most prominent African American authors of his time without having ever relied on a larger, more-established publishing company.

He is the recipient of fellowships from both the National Endowment for the Arts and the National Endowment for the Humanities. In 1984 he was presented with the Distinguished Writers Award from the Middle Atlantic Writers Association. He is also the 1993 recipient of the Paul Robeson Award from the African-American Arts Alliance.

Madhubuti has published several collections of poetry, including *Think Black, Black Pride, We Walk the Way of the World, Direction score: Selected and New Poems, Book of Life* and *Don't Cry, Scream*. In addition to his poetry collections, Madhubuti also published a collection of critical essays entitled, *Dynamite Voices: Black poets* of the 1960s.

Madhubuti continues to write and is the Director of the Gwendolyn Brooks Center at Chicago State University where he resides with his wife Safisha.

Karen Quinones Miller

Karen Quinones Miller's first novel, *Satin Doll,* was self-published in 1999. After embarking on a major marketing campaign, she secured a publishing contract with Simon and Schuster for a series of novels, which includes the revised *Satin Doll* (2001), *I'm Telling* (2002), *Using What You Got* (2003) and *Ida B* (2004).

Born and raised in Harlem, Karen dropped out of school at the age of 13, and spent the majority of her teenage years experiencing street life first-hand. After a tour of duty in the Navy, the birth of her daughter and a divorce, Karen moved to Philadelphia.

Ms. Miller enrolled at Temple University and began working as a correspondent for *The Philadelphia New Observer*—a weekly African American newspaper. She graduated magna cum laude from Temple with a B.A. in journalism

In 1994, Karen started her first permanent job at The Virginian-Pilot Norfolk, Va. Less than a year later she left to join The Philadelphia Inquirer as a staff writer at covering West Philadelphia.

Now, a full-time novelist, Ms. Miller currently lives in Philadelphia.

Mary Morrison

Ms. Morrison is an author, poet and lecturer. She began writing poetry in 1983 and began reciting her poems publicly in 1988. Mary woke up one morning, in 1999, and decided it was time for her to step out on faith. It was time to stop talking about her dream and start living her dream to become a critically acclaimed best-selling author. Author of *Justice Just Us Just Me*, her first book of poetry was self-published August 23, 1999.

Mary didn't realize she wanted to be a writer until after she completed her first novel, *Soul Mates Dissipate.* The title, *Soul Mates Dissipate* remained the same for seven long years. Today it's no longer just a dream, it's a national Essence and Blackboard Bestseller!

After working for the government for 18 years, Mary quit her job on June 3, 2000, and never looked back. Before she resigned, Mary laid the four month foundation and wrote her novel at night and on the weekends, simultaneously caring for her son.

Mary ordered 11,000 copies of Soul Mates Dissipate and had them delivered to the front door of her townhouse on May 25, 2000. She rolled up her sleeves and marched side-by-side with her publicist, Felicia Polk, and journeyed on a 25-city tour across America starting with BookExpo America (BEA) in Chicago, Illinois on May 30, 2000. At BEA, copies of the novel were personally handed to agents, booksellers, authors, and publishers. Five months later, all 11,000 copies were sold!

On the first round of queries for Soul Mates Dissipate, within four weeks, her newly-acquired agent Claudia Menza landed Mary a six-figure, three book deal with Kensington Publishing Corporation in New York City. Mary was born in Aurora, Illinois, reared in New Orleans, Louisiana, and currently resides in the Oakland, CA.

Victoria Christopher Murray

Victoria Christopher Murray always knew she would become an author, even as she was taking quite an unlikely path to that destination. A native of Queens, New York, Victoria first left New York to attend Hampton Institute in Virginia where she majored in Communication Disorders. After graduating in 1977, Victoria attended New York University where she received her Master of Business Administration in 1979.

Victoria spent ten years in Corporate America before she decided to test her entrepreneurial spirit. Having never lost the dream to write Victoria originally self published *Temptation* in 1997.

It had been a long road before my agent was able to find a publisher; but in 2000, Warner Books picked up a contract to publish *Temptation* on their Walk Worthy Press imprint. *Temptation* has made numerous best sellers' lists including Emerge and The Dallas/Fort Worth Morning News and remained on the *Essence bestsellers* list for nine consecutive months. It was also was nominated in 2001 for an NAACP Image Award in Outstanding Literature.

Victoria's second novel *Joy* was released in October 2001. *Joy* has also been an Essence bestseller and won the 2002 Gold Pen Award for Best Inspirational Fiction. Her third novel is Truth Be Told (2004).

In 2003, Victoria joined with five authors for the first Christian fiction anthology. Blessed Assurance is a collection of short stories where each author chose a character from the Bible and brought their story into 2003.

Ms. Murray is an Associate Editor with *Black Issues Book Review* and a contributor to *Quarterly Black Review*. She lives in Inglewood, California.

Kimberla Lawson Roby

Kimberla Lawson Roby is author of the critically acclaimed, best-selling novels *Casting the First Stone, Here and Now,* and her debut title, *Behind Closed Doors*, which was originally self-published through her own company, Lenox Press.

Ms. Roby's novels have frequented numerous bestseller lists, including *Essence Magazine* and *Emerge Magazine* and placed #1 Blackboard bestsellers for four consecutive months in 1997 and 2000 respectively. In addition, Ms. Roby's first novel was nominated for Blackboard's 1998 and 1999 Fiction Book of the Year Award, and she received the 1998 First-Time Author Award from Chicago's Black History Month Book Fair and Conference.

Roby began her career in 1996 when she self-published her debut novel, *Behind Closed Doors*, and sold 10,000 copies within the first six months. Following her success, the best-selling author, received bids from several major New York publishers.

Her fourth novel, *It's a Thin Line*, was published by Kensington Press (2001), followed by *Casting the First Stone* (2002). Ms. Robie later signed with William Morrow, a division of Harper Collins, which has since published *A Taste of Reality* (2003) and *Too Much of a Good Thing* (2004)

Tony Rose

For Tony Rose, Publisher and CEO of Amber Communications Group, Inc. (Amber, Busta, Colossus, Ambrosia and Amber/Wiley Books (WWW.AMBERBOOKS.COM) the road entering the publishing world has been long, with many twists and turns.

He grew up in a Boston housing project where the environment was violent, and where he learned to escape through reading many books. His passion for the written word evolved through the many writing competitions that he would win during his school years.

After completing a tour of duty in the Air Force, Mr. Rose went to UCLA to study journalism. However, while in Los Angeles, he was drafted into the music industry and embarked on what would be a 20 year stint heading up his successful international music production business.

In 1998, when he sold the music business, Mr. Rose invested in his first passion—books. What had been planned as a one book "self-publishing" effort, with *Is Modeling for You? The Handbook and Guide for the Young Aspiring Black Model,* the book he co-write with his wife, Yvonne Rose, is still thriving six years and thirty-two books later.

Rose attributes his success to the many African-American bookstores that supported his efforts when he started out, and fondly remembers his first sale to Brother Nati of Afrikan World Books who bought a caseload at the IBBMEC. In 2002, the company was incorporated as AMBER COMMUNICATIONS GROUP, INC. (ACGI)

ACGI's first imprint AMBER BOOKS is the nation's largest African-American self-help and career guide publishing house and the recipient of the Chicago Black Book Fair and Conference Independent Publisher/Press Award of the Year, the 2003 BlackBoard Bestseller's African-American Publisher of the Year Award and the 2003 American Library Association Reluctant Reader Award. The Company continues to expand with its celebrity bio imprint BUSTA BOOKS, its COLOSSUS BOOKS imprint for international personalities and topics, its AMBROSIA BOOKS imprint for great literature, fiction and non-fiction, and AMBER/ WILEY'S co-publishing/imprint deal with John Wiley & Sons, Inc. for personal finance and beauty books. Currently five Amber Book titles and three Amber/Wiley titles reside at the Bookspan's *Black Expressions* Book Club, the nation's largest African-American Book Club.

Brenda Thomas

Brenda Thomas came up through the ranks of the business world as a career secretary and administrator. After spending 12 years at IBM, she began her own administrative and marketing consulting firm, Admin Ink, through which she continues to provide support to professionals in various industries.

After years in the corporate sector, she took a position at AND 1 Basketball, as its Manager of Product Placement and Player Relations. In this position, she worked to place AND 1 product on television sitcoms, movies, celebrities and athletes. She also coordinated appearances for their seven NBA players, as well as providing game shoes and other apparel until Stephon X. Marbury asked her to be on his team exclusively, as his personal assistant.

Throughout her adult life, she has maintained her passion for writing—it was born from her love of reading as well as her desire to pass on her life stories and lessons to others. Her first novel, *Threesome: Where Seduction, Power and Basketball Collide* and its sequel *Fourplay: The Dance of Sensuality*, reflect some of those experiences.

Brenda has now dedicated herself exclusively to writing. Her next project is a short story, *Maxed Out*, which will be included in the anthology titled, *Four Degrees of Heat*. She is currently working on her next full-length novel titled, *The Velvet Rope*, to be released in November 2004.

In 2001 Brenda self-published *Threesome* with WritersandPoets.com. She launched a major promotional campaign, beginning at Book Expo America and soon had a national bestseller. Thomas has appeared on Dateline NBC, Fox, Court TV, CNN Entertainment Tonight and dozens of radio and talk shows in the US and Canada.

You can usually find Brenda at home in Philadelphia where she resides with her two children, three granddaughters and a wealth of family and friends. Soon after, Pocket Books (a division of Simon & Schuster) offered Brenda a publishing deal and released her second novel *Fourplay* in April 2004. (www.phillywriter.com)

Omar Tyree

In 1989, Tyree attended Howard University and began a new career interest in writing. In his senior year in 1991, he became the first student in Howard University history to have a featured column, "Food For Thought," published in The Hilltop, the school's award-winning newspaper. Following the completion of undergraduate studies in December of 1991, he was hired as a reporter and an assistant editor at The Capital Spotlight weekly newspaper in Washington, D.C., where he also sold advertising. He later served as the chief reporter for News Dimensions weekly newspaper while freelancing for the Washington View Magazine.

Tyree made his next move writing and publishing books. After having first hand experience with print shops and typesetting at newspaper plants, he organized MARS Productions, a sole-proprietorship, to publish his first novel, "Colored, On White Campus." The small-scale book was published in October of 1992, with financial help from friends and family, who offered him personal loans. "Colored, On White Campus" sold well enough to produce funds to publish his second effort, *Flyy Girl* in April of 1993. By July of 1993, Omar Tyree was self-employed.

"*Capital City: The Chronicles of a D.C. Underworld*," was released in April of 1994, becoming Tyree's third successfully published book. In January of 1995, he republished "*Colored, On White Campus*" as "*BattleZone: The Struggle to Survive the American Institution*" with a new cover design. He was also published in a Beacon Press release entitled "*Testimony: Young African-Americans on Self-Discovery and Black Identity*" in February of 1995.

His three published books, "*Flyy-Girl*," "*Capital City*" and "*BattleZone*" have all been picked up by book distributors in New York, New Jersey, Atlanta, Virginia, Baltimore and Chicago. Sales escalated to more than 25,000 copies, and are still selling rapidly through Tyree's of persistence in marketing.

In August of 1995, author Omar Tyree was picked up on a two-book contract deal, which included the republication of "*Flyy Girl*" in hardback form, by the major publishing house of Simon & Schuster.

Other published novels by Omar Tyree include: *Single Mom* (1999), *Sweet St. Louis* (1999), *A Do Right Man* (1998), *For The Love of Money* (2001), *Leslie* (2002), *Just Say No* (2002), *Diary of a Groupie* (2003).

He won the 2001 NAACP Image Award for Literary Fiction.

Omar Tyree was born and raised in Philadelphia, Pennsylvania, and presently lives in New Castle Delaware.

Carl Weber

Carl Weber started in the book publishing industry as the owner and operator of three bookstores in New York City. The three stores bear the name, African-American Bookstore, and can be found in Queens, Brooklyn, or Long Island. Weber always wanted to own his own business, but didn't know that it would be books.

As a bookseller, Carl realized that African-American commercial fiction was an upcoming market. In hopes of becoming part of that movement Weber decided that he too would write relationship novels from a male perspective, one that told the other side of the story for ordinary brothers out there searching for love ("Sister-Girl" novels).

In one year Carl completed his first novel *Lookin for Luv*, which was published in September 2000. Using his connections within the publishing industry Weber had managed to have his book picked up by Dafina Books imprint in less than three months, as part of a major publishing deal with Kensington's new romance division. *Lookin for Luv*, like Weber's second novel *Married Men* (published September 2001), is a relationship novel written from the perspective of an African-American male searching for love in untraditional places.

Other novels by best-selling author Carl Weber include: *Baby Momma Drama* (2004) and *Player Haters* (2004). Mr. Weber has also compiled two books of short stories, also published by Dafina Books—*A Dollar and a Dream* (2003) and *Around the Way Girls* (2004) - written with authors Angel Hunter, Jill Hunt, and Dwayne S. Joseph.

Zane

The National Bestselling Author, Zane has made the Essence list more than half a dozen times and has had the distinguished honor of having her first three books make the top five in a single month.

Zane is the Principal/Publisher of Strebor Books International LLC, an emerging African American publishing house with more than a dozen authors, founded in 1999.

Since then, Strebor has produced numerous bestsellers, including the three novels that Zane originally self-published: *The Sex Chronicles: Shattering the Myth, Addicted* and *Shame on it All*

Zane signed with Simon & Schuster for the re-release of Addicted on their Pocket Books imprint in 2002. Since that time, she has had several books published on Simon & Schuster's various imprints, including: *The Sex Chronicles: Shattering the Myth* (2002), *Skyscraper* (2003), *Nervous* (2003) and *Chocoalte Flava: The Eroticanoir.com Anthology* (2004)

Index

About the Author

Takesha Powell, a New York City native is the former Managing Editor of *Black Elegance* and *Belle* magazines as well as former Editor-in-Chief of *Jive/Intimacy* magazines.

Ms. Powell has two self-published books: an anthology of poetry entitled *Tender Headed: Poems For Nappy Thoughts I Left Uncombed*, and a novel, *The Goode Sisters*. Her next work, *The Sisterhood Commandments: A Novella* is due for release August 2005.

She resides both in New York and New Jersey with her daughter.